Capacity Management

IT Infrastructure Library

Brian Johnson

LONDON: THE STATIONERY OFFICE

Published for the Central Computer and Telecommunications Agency under licence from the Controller of Her Majesty's Stationery Office.

First published 1991
Eighth impression 2000

ISBN 0 11 330544 3

This is one of the books published in the IT Infrastructure Library series.

For further information on other CCTA products, contact:

CCTA Library,
Rosebery Court,
St Andrews Court Business Park
Norwich, NR7 0HS

This document has been produced using procedures conforming to
BSI 5750 Part 1: 1987; ISO 9001:1987.

Table of contents

Foreword

Welcome to the IT Infrastructure Library module on **Capacity Management.**

In their respective areas the IT Infrastructure Library publications complement and provide more detail than the IS Guides.

The ethos behind the development of the IT Infrastructure Library is the recognition that organizations are becoming increasingly dependent on IT in order to satisfy their corporate aims and meet their business needs. This growing dependency leads to growing requirement for quality IT services. In this context quality means 'matched to business needs and user requirements as these evolve'.

This module is one of a series of codes of practice intended to facilitate the quality management of IT services and of the IT Infrastructure. (By IT Infrastructure, we mean organizations' computers and networks - hardware, software and computer related communications, upon which application systems and IT services are built and run). The codes of practice will assist organizations to provide quality IT services in the face of skill shortages, system complexity, rapid change, growing user expectations, current and future user requirements.

Underpinning the IT Infrastructure is the Environmental Infrastructure upon which it is built. Environmental topics are covered in separate sets of guides within the IT Infrastructure Library.

IT infrastructure management is a complex subject which for presentational and practical reasons has been broken down within the IT Infrastructure Library into a series of modules. A complete list of current and planned modules is available from the CCTA IT Infrastructure Management Services at the address given at the back of this module.

The structure of the module is, in essence:

* a **Management summary** aimed at senior managers (Directors of IT and above, typically down to Civil Service Grade 5), senior IT staff and, in some cases, users or office managers (typically Civil Service Grades 5 to 7)
* the main body of the text, aimed at IT middle management (typically grades 7 to HEO)
* technical detail in Annexes.

The module gives the main **guidance** in sections 3 to 5; explains the **benefits, costs and possible problems** in section 6, which may be of interest to senior staff; and provides information on **tools** (requirements and examples of real-life availability) in section 7.

CCTA is working with the IT industry to foster the development of software tools to underpin the guidance contained within the codes of practice (ie to make adherence to the module more practicable), and ultimately to automate functions.

If you have any comments on this or other modules, do please let us know. A **Comments sheet** is provided with every module. Alternatively you may wish to contact us directly using the reference point given in **Further information**.

Thank you. We hope you find this module useful.

Acknowledgements

The assistance of the following contributors is gratefully acknowledged.

Brian King (under contract to CCTA from LOGICA).

Simon Furey (under contract to CCTA from LOGICA).

Hans Dithmar (under contract to CCTA from CCMS Ltd).

The assistance of Roy Longbottom, (Principal Performance Engineer, CCTA), is also gratefully acknowledged.

1. Management summary

1.1 Background

In some quarters, it has become fashionable to say that, because the cost of hardware is coming down, it is cheaper to 'buy a bigger box and forget capacity management'. This statement is not simply untrue, but dangerous. Capacity management should not be reactive; capacity management is about no surprises, no urgent purchases of hardware. Good capacity management will enable an organization to manage resources in times of crisis and predict the need for additional hardware in advance.

Capacity management is a key element in the provision of quality IT services - the provision of these services to meet evolving business needs on time, at minimum cost. The techniques of capacity management enable an organization to use existing capacity economically and effectively, and provides the essential planning information in support of a sound investment plan that is compatible with the IS strategy of the organization.

1.2 Capacity management

Capacity management is an essential function in enabling an organization's IT Directorate to:

* meet customers' requirements for
    - transaction volumes and turnaround times
    - resilience (to meet Service Level Agreements)
    - terminal response times
* support the changing portfolio of application systems that are needed by the organization's businesses as they evolve.

Capacity management is concerned with having the appropriate IT capacity and with making best use of it. Capacity management embraces the following functions:

* planning to ensure that cost-justifiable capacity always exists to process the workloads agreed between the IT Directorate and supported businesses and to provide the required performance quality and quantity

* monitoring the IT systems used and the services provided, to check that the work can be processed and the performance levels experienced are as specified in Service Level Agreements (SLAs), and recommending corrective action if they are not
* identifying the work and the levels of service that can be supported on available or planned capacity
* using capacity in an optimum way.

1.3 Benefits

Capacity management results in cost savings by ensuring that:

* capacity is closely matched to requirements (and that enhancements to capacity match projected business need)
* better service results in more efficient use of IT by business users
* available capacity is used efficiently.

Capacity management reduces the risk that the IT Directorate might fail to support evolving business needs through lack of capacity: new customers and new or changed applications can be supported with confidence that there is adequate capacity.

Capacity management also contributes to good customer relations, ensuring the services are consistent and in accord with the appropriate SLA.

1.4 About this module

This module describes the processes involved in planning, implementing and running a capacity management function. Advice is given on how to cost-justify the creation of a capacity management function. Section 6 provides a more detailed description of the benefits which can be achieved.

2. Introduction

2.1 Purpose

Capacity management is needed to support the optimum and cost-effective provision of IT services by helping organizations to match their IT resources to the demands of their business.

The purpose of this module is to provide guidance to organizations on how to justify and establish a capacity management function, and the procedures necessary for the planning, implementation and running of that function.

2.2 Target readership

This module of the IT Infrastructure Library is aimed at IT Services Managers, Capacity Managers, Telecommunications Managers, Network Managers, Computer Operations Managers and Service Level Managers, and at the staff who work for these managers.

2.3 Scope

This module covers all aspects of capacity management - planning, implementation, post-implementation review and ongoing operation - for both host (mainframe) and data networks.

The subjects of downsizing and UNIX capacity management are not covered, because there is not yet sufficient detailed information available in what are currently, highly volatile areas. A number of enlightened organizations are examining UNIX and downsizing, but good, sound and tested practices may not emerge for some time.

Computer capacity management and network capacity management are similar in purpose and have some similarities in function. Where the overlap of responsibilities is significant or the methods used are similar, combined sections are used within this module. Elsewhere, where differences between the two tasks warrant different treatment, separate sections are used.

The capacity management tasks in these two areas are frequently assigned to people with differing backgrounds and expertise - in host computers and telecommunications respectively. This module covers the coordination of the efforts of the people from these two disciplines.

The guidance in the module is directly applicable to mainframes, minicomputers and networks. Annex K describes how the guidance can be adapted for microcomputers.

The guidance in the module applies primarily to the capacity management of existing sites and systems. However, the guidance can also be applied to greenfield sites - see Annex J for more details.

2.3.1 Elements of capacity management

Figure 1, opposite, outlines the main elements of capacity management as covered by this module, and the flow of data and information.

A brief description of each of the elements of capacity management which are shown in figure 1 follows. Guidance on the workings of these elements is given later in the module.

Note that it is neither feasible nor desirable to implement all these elements of capacity management in a single phase - rather, implement the elements in a phased manner. See section 4.1.9 for guidance on implementing capacity management.

Performance management is concerned with the monitoring and tuning of existing system(s) to ensure that optimum use is made of the hardware resources, and that agreed performance and throughput levels can be achieved and maintained.

Capacity Management Database (CDB) creation and reporting deals with the collection and maintenance of all technical, business, and ancillary data which is required for capacity management and with the production of reports which are required from the CDB.

Workload management is concerned with identifying and understanding the applications, their work patterns and peaks, and their use of hardware resources. The information gathered is used by the capacity planner to:

* estimate future demand
* forecast the likely use of hardware resources
* forecast expected performance and throughput levels.

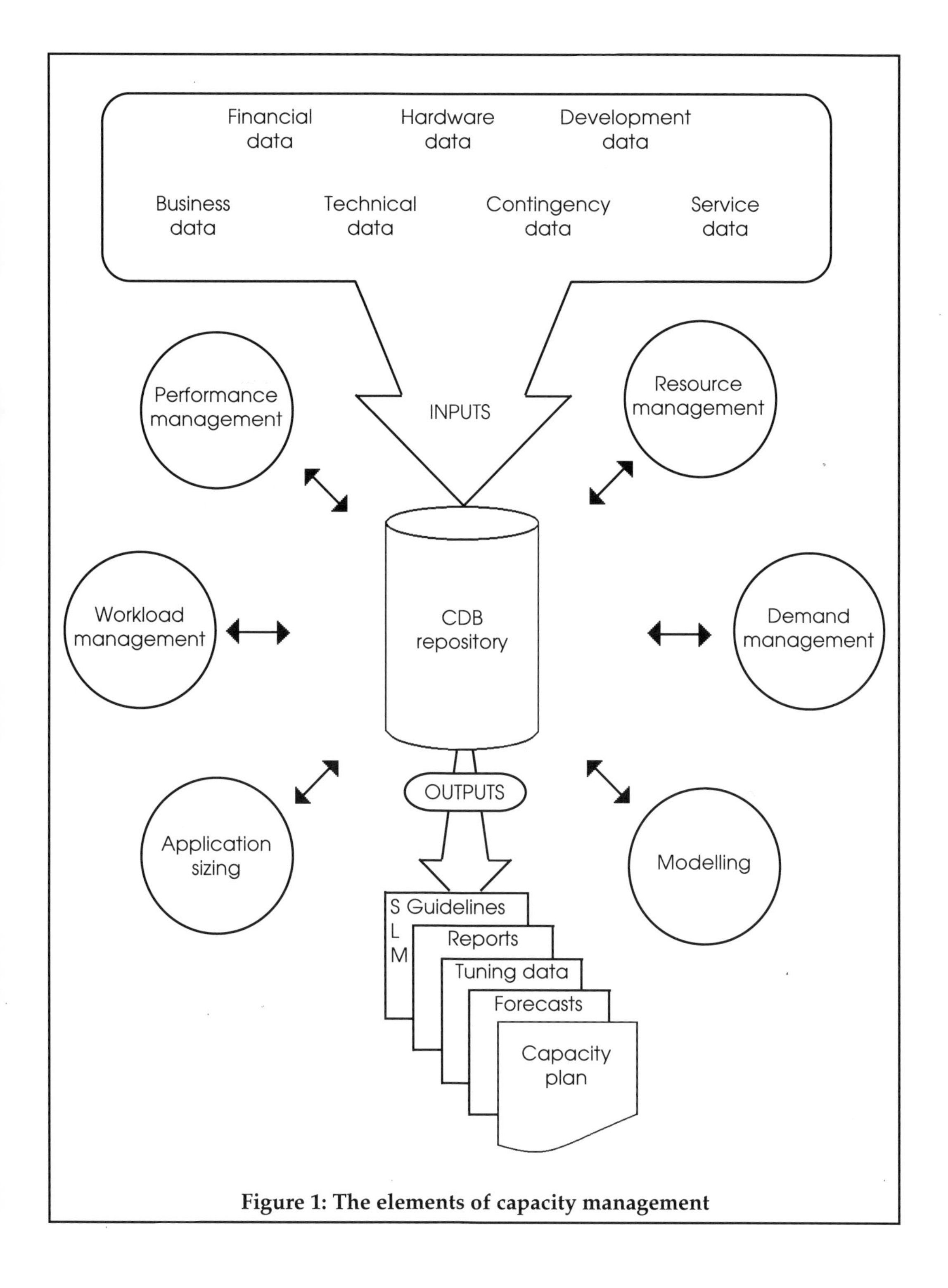

Figure 1: The elements of capacity management

Application sizing forecasts the hardware resources required for new applications which are currently being developed, and the expected performance and throughput levels and any cost implications (for hardware).

Production of the capacity plan covers production of the major deliverable of the capacity management system. The capacity plan is a statement of the hardware resources (and associated costs) which will be required to meet the agreed service levels for performance and throughput up to the agreed planning horizon.

Resource management covers a number of activities, such as storage management (responsibility for the allocation and the control of filestore), the assessment of new hardware technology and, in collaboration with other IT services sections, planning for resilience and recovering from disasters that may affect IT services.

Demand management covers the management of users' demands for IT resources either as a short-term expedient because there is insufficient capacity to support the work being run and at the same time provide agreed service levels or, as a deliberate instrument of IT management policy, to reduce the required capacity in the longer term. In both cases the workloads run are affected; in the latter case, the capacity plan is also affected.

2.4 Related guidance

This book is one of a series of modules which are issued as part of the IT Infrastructure Library (ITIL). Although this module can be read in isolation, it should be used in conjunction with the other modules. The following IT Infrastructure Library modules have particular relevance.

The **Service Level Management** module describes how Service Level Agreements (SLAs) should be negotiated with users for the levels of service that IT Services will provide, and how those agreements should subsequently be implemented, monitored and reviewed. The Capacity Manager is responsible for advising the Service Level Manager about achievable levels of performance and throughput which can be put into SLAs, and for the implementation of a system to monitor actual performance and throughput levels.

The **Application Lifecycle Support** module gives guidance on the responsibilities of IT Services management regarding application development projects and the subsequent live running, maintenance and enhancement of applications software. The Capacity Manager must liaise with the project team to size the hardware resources which will be required to run the new applications and to meet service level commitments, while ensuring that the service levels of existing systems can be maintained. The Capacity Manager advises on the implications of the proposed design of the application with respect to optimum use of hardware resources, plus all cost and service level implications.

The **Availability Management** module covers the planning and ongoing management activities which are needed to ensure that the reliability and availability levels, as specified in service level agreements, are achieved and maintained. Capacity management complements availability management to ensure systems are planned and managed to meet both capacity/performance and availability/reliability requirements.

The **Configuration Management, Change Management** and **Problem Management** modules explain the important processes that are needed to maintain quality IT services in the face of changes and problems. Capacity management needs to assess the impact of proposed and implemented changes on performance and capacity. Any changes that capacity management wishes to initiate should be submitted to the change management system for authorization. Performance problems are recorded on the problem management system, for resolution by capacity management.

The **Contingency Planning** module gives guidance on the processes which facilitate recovery from any partial or complete loss of the service. The capacity management team must define the backup hardware resources which are required to support those applications which have been identified as essential, with due consideration to SLA and cost implications.

The module **Cost Management for IT Services** describes all aspects of the costing of, and optionally charging for, IT services. Capacity management is closely involved in the provision of resource usage data which is used in cost management. In addition, capacity plans feed into the cost plans.

The **Network Management** module gives guidance on the overall planning and control of telecommunications facilities. This module should be read in order to put network capacity management in perspective as a function of network management.

The **Vendor Management** module gives guidance on managing the IT Directorate's relationship with IT suppliers and maintainers. On detailed issues relating to the performance of vendor products (hardware and software) the Capacity Manager is the organization's technical authority.

The IT Infrastructure Library Environmental Sets outline issues affecting the provision of accommodation and environmental facilities for IT. The modules **Specification and Management of a Cable Infrastructure** and **Accommodation Specification** are particularly relevant to capacity management.

2.5 Standards

The following standards are applicable in the area of capacity management.

SSADM - Structured Systems Analysis and Design Method

SSADM is the recommended standard systems analysis and design method used for application development in government. SSADM provides the information which capacity management requires to size the hardware resources needed to support new applications and meet SLAs.

ISO 9001/EN29000/BS5750 - Quality management and quality assurance standards

The IT Infrastructure Library modules are being designed to assist adherents to obtain third-party quality certification to ISO 9001. CCTA recommends that Facilities Management (FM) providers are required to use the principles set out in the IT Infrastructure Library modules and that the FM provider's IT infrastructure/service management procedures are certified by a third-party certification body to ISO 9001. Such third parties should be accredited by the NACCB, the National Accreditation Council for Certification Bodies.

Data communications standards

There are many standards within the subject of data communications, either *de jure* (for example the Government OSI Profile, GOSIP) or *de facto* (for example IBM's Systems Network Architecture, SNA).

Capacity Managers must be familiar with:

* the characteristics and limitations of existing standards such as X.25 - an understanding of this topic is required for realistic performance expectations and to make sustainable service predictions
* the ways to relate the various standards for efficient interworking of network components
* the timetable for the inception of new standards which may affect the timing of equipment procurement and thus the network capacity
* areas where there are current gaps in the standards and where proprietary solutions may be needed to provide short-term capacity or capacity management facilities
* the standard options that are available for providing network capacity, eg line speeds.

Familiarity with the CCITT X and V series recommendations and the OSI 7-layer model is essential.

There are no standards relating to the process of network capacity management.

3. Planning for capacity management

This section gives guidance on planning for capacity management. The section covers the following activities:

* appoint a Capacity Manager (3.1.1)
* produce a mission statement (3.1.2)
* use of PRINCE (3.1.3)
* initiate a feasibility study (3.1.4)
* review current systems (3.1.5)
* perform a gap analysis (3.1.6)
* produce a project plan for creating or improving the capacity management function (3.1.7)
* development and implementation study (3.1.8)
* define the roles, responsibilities and requirements for staff (3.1.9)
* select support tools (3.1.10)
* define accommodation and environmental requirements (3.1.11).

Separation of mainframe and network capacity management

Capacity management functions for the host computer and the network are similar in purpose and have some similarities in function. However, the respective capacity management tasks are frequently assigned to people of differing backgrounds and expertise, those of mainframes and telecommunications respectively. Therefore, the first decision which must be made is whether it is sensible to bring them together under a unified capacity management function or keep them as two discrete roles. In IT organizations which employ less than 100 staff, it is recommended that a single function is installed. In larger sites, the mainframe and network elements should be separated although both could report to one Capacity Manager.

It is likely that a team of staff will be needed in large organizations.

3.1 Procedures

3.1.1 Appoint a Capacity Manager

Appoint a Capacity Manager who will be responsible for the capacity management function. The post normally resides within the IT services area. For all but the very smallest computer installations and networks, regard the role of Capacity Manager as a full-time job.

The Capacity Manager's main responsibilities in order of importance, are likely to be as follows, to:

* produce capacity plans with a forward window far enough ahead to take account of changes to IT capacity (which fit in with the organization's business planning cycle) and that document the need for any hardware upgrades or additional equipment, based on service level requirements, cost constraints, reliability and availability

* produce regular management reports which include current usage of resources, trends and forecasts

* size proposed new systems, including for example bespoke applications, packages, decision support systems, and office systems with respect to the computer and network resources required, to determine hardware utilizations, performance service levels and cost implications

* assess new technology and its relevance to the organization in terms of performance and cost

* implement a service level reporting system

* maintain a knowledge of future demand for IT services and predict the effects of that demand on service levels

* determine service levels that are maintainable and cost-justified

* carry out performance testing of new systems

* recommend tuning, where practical, and make recommendations to IT management customers on the design and use of systems to help ensure optimum use is made of all hardware and operating software resources

* recommend resolutions to performance problems
* recommend to IT Services management when to employ demand management techniques (to dampen user demands on the systems)
* carry out *ad hoc* studies in the area of capacity management on request from IT management.

For guidance on the qualities required of a Capacity Manager, please refer to section 3.3.1.

3.1.2 Produce a mission statement

In order to clarify the objectives of the capacity management function, a simple mission statement should be defined. The mission statement should describe the reason for implementing or improving the capacity management system. Documenting this will help to ensure that other members of the organization understand the overall goal.

The mission statement given below is an example which can be used or adapted to the requirements of the organization.

> "To ensure that cost justifiable IT capacity always exists which is matched to the needs of the supported business".

Ideally the mission statement should be no more than a sentence, so that it is quickly and easily understood.

3.1.3 Use of PRINCE

It is recommended that all of the work necessary in the design of a capacity management system is managed according to the PRINCE (PRojects IN a Controlled Environment) method.

Essentially, use of PRINCE will divide the work into separate projects:

* feasibility study
* development and implementation study.

Project board

To manage the projects, PRINCE recommends the creation of a project board to oversee the work.

A project board will generally comprise:

* Executive: the director of IS in the organization
* Senior User: a senior manager from the business community
* Senior Technical: the project manager of the feasibility and development/ implementation studies.

The project board must make business decisions based on the recommendations of the project team's feasibility study and also set meaningful budgets for the development/ implementation project.

The project board will appoint a project manager and, amongst other things, the project manager will decide on the team structure needed to manage the projects.

Project management

The project manager will be present throughout the feasibility, development and implementation phases of capacity management.

The overall terms of reference for the project manager include:

* quality objectives
* development of plans
* performance indicators
* assessment of the cost of quality.

The project manager is responsible for:

* definition of responsibilities for the team
* preparation of Project and Stage level plans
* setting objectives for the stage managers
* scheduling of control points
* creation of a configuration management structure (guidance is available in the IT Infrastructure Library **Configuration Management** module)
* preparation of periodic highlight reports
* presentations at mid-stage and end-stage assessment meetings

* enforcement of technical exception procedures
* preparation of exception plans.

More guidance about these procedures can be found in the appropriate PRINCE publications.

The project manager will appoint a Capacity Manager (or Managers) to act as chief architect of any proposed capacity management systems. The Capacity Manager should be appointed prior to commencing the feasibility study.

Support staff will be needed prior to implementation of capacity management.

3.1.4 Initiate a feasibility study

Because of the variety of components making up capacity management (performance, modelling, sizing and so on) it is sometimes difficult to identify what should be included in the feasibility study. In general it is best confined to examining whether:

* capacity management is currently practised, and if so, to what extent
* introduction of capacity management is likely to be cost effective and would bring improvements
* staff are available
* there is management commitment to introduction of capacity management.

Capacity management is a vital function: a feasibility study for its introduction should therefore focus on the positive effects of introducing the function and examine what it is that the organization will achieve through operating a capacity management function.

The feasibility study is best split into four component parts:

* produce a framework description for introduction or improvement of capacity management
* review the current systems
* perform a gap analysis
* produce a management report, for creating or improving capacity management.

Framework description

Produce a framework description for the introduction or improvement of the capacity management function. The framework description should be based on the mission statement and is, in effect, a business case describing the desired state of the capacity management function in some detail. The benefits to the business should be highlighted for senior management. Furthermore it should outline requirements, a project plan and costs. The framework description will almost certainly become the feasibility study report.

The framework description should as a minimum describe:

* roles and responsibilities of staff involved with capacity management
* procedures specifying the operation of capacity management
* interfaces and procedures relating to other IT management areas to define the scope of the function
* IT management information required from capacity management to assess the effectiveness and efficiency of the capacity management function
* accommodation and environment requirements
* an outline project plan, stating activities, end-products, controls, organization and required resources
* budgetary estimates of expenditure based on the outline project plan
* the contents of the capacity management database (CDB). The description should cover both technical and business-related data
* expectations of regular and exception reporting facilities required from monitoring tools and the CDB at the operational, tactical and strategic levels, also the information required by and presented to the cost management function
* the current status and expected development of Service Level Agreements, service objectives and performance criteria, ie does the organization adhere to, or intend to adhere to SLAs

* scope of the capacity management function in the technical sense, ie does the capacity management function cover hardware, networks, system software, application software, in-house developed application software.

Current systems review

Where capacity management is practised in the organization begin with a review to firmly establish details of the procedures, processes and tools. These details are required to enable analysis of the gap between the required functionality and the current functionality. The review should be sufficiently detailed to allow a detailed project plan to be established.

The review should address the following topics:

* the procedures currently in place and their effectiveness
* who is responsible for existing capacity management activities (if any)
* the tools currently in use and their effectiveness
* current customer satisfaction with the present situation; focus on those users most affected, ie those users with the most stringent performance requirements and those users with the largest demand for capacity
* current and desired requirements by other IT Services management areas, such as service level management, availability and cost management
* current budget and cost effectiveness.

Gap analysis

The gap analysis should:

* identify the major differences between the current functionality and the required functionality of the capacity management function
* if the gap between the current and the required functionality is large, identify separate phases, specifying required functionality, staff, procedures and support tools. Each step can then be treated as a separate project.

For each detailed step a separate description of the functionality required has to be produced. Due to the technical nature of the subject, the following division in steps is recommended:

* identifying workloads
* measuring and understanding workloads
* generating workload forecasts
* basic performance management and tuning (be aware that this is to gain a basic understanding; a warning should be applied here since it is very easy to allow performance management issues to take up all of the available time)
* construction of the host and network capacity management databases
* exception reporting
* establishing initial service levels or service level objectives; these are not to be included in Service Level Agreements
* production of the capacity plan.

Produce management report

Now produce a management report (based on the framework description, current systems review and gap analysis) to conclude the feasibility study. Submit the feasibility study report to the IT Services Manager and to the project board for approval. The report should include:

* an assessment of the current situation with regard to the services which are being provided, and to capacity management
* a statement of all problems which need to be addressed, eg lack of communication, lack of relevant information or capacity
* the need for capacity management within the organization and the benefits which can be expected (section 6 gives guidance on this subject). Note that it does not necessarily follow that capacity management will be required by all organizations. That is, if service levels are not important, growth is non-existent, cost is not an issue, or the organization has implicit faith in its suppliers then maybe capacity management is not necessary

* recommendations on how to implement capacity management within the organization (this section should include any prerequisites or constraints in terms of organizational structure or culture)
* examples of prototype reports which could be produced by capacity management to stimulate reaction
* a project plan, showing timescales, staffing levels, costs (section 4.1.9 gives guidance on the order in which tasks should be tackled) and specifying the objectives, main tasks, ongoing operations and deliverables of each phase.

3.1.5 The development and implementation study

Following management approval of the feasibility study, the initial task for the appointed Capacity Manager is to perform a study to plan the development and implementation of capacity management.

The size and scope of the study depends on the size of the IT Directorate: remember it is often best to implement capacity management as a series of discrete projects, each having its own objectives, tasks and deliverables.

Terms of reference

The IT Services Manager should draw up terms of reference for this study. For example:

Objectives

* to establish the need for capacity management in the organization
* to quantify the costs and the benefits which can be expected from the implementation of capacity management
* make recommendations as to how capacity management can be successfully implemented and managed within the organization.

Method

Meet the objectives by:

* obtaining a good understanding of the organization, its business objectives, and service level requirements, the IT applications, hardware resources and communications facilities

* identifying any problems or risks arising from the introduction of capacity management
* identifying the risks to the organization of failing to introduce capacity management
* establishing the current status of any existing work in the area of capacity management
* identifying any current problems which may affect the successful implementation of capacity management. This activity should include the identification of those problems that capacity management can help to resolve, eg poor service, lack of planning, and inadequate communication. The Capacity Manager should address those problems which need to be resolved as a prerequisite to the implementation of capacity management; eg lack of commitment, poor understanding of service level objectives, development standards which provide little or no sizing information on new applications
* evaluating the tools which are applicable
* producing a detailed project plan for the implementation of capacity management, showing objectives, tasks, deliverables, timescales, staffing and costs.

Deliverables

The main deliverable is a written report which details all findings, recommendations on implementation, project plans and costs.

In addition, it will be necessary to present the findings formally to the Project Board.

Meetings

Regard meetings as an opportunity to exchange views and information. Do not consider them to be a one-way collection of information, ie an interview. Arrange meetings with the people listed below. As a preamble to the meeting the Capacity Manager should explain, in terms which are appropriate to the other party, what the objectives of capacity management are, and what benefits it will bring to the organization in general and to that person in particular.

Some of the items below can be viewed as being part of the implementation itself, rather than of the planning process. However, these items are covered to provide solid background material in order to understand the full implications of capacity management for the organization. This appreciation of the scope of the work allows the Capacity Manager to produce a more realistic project plan. Production of a responsibilities matrix would be especially useful in this task.

The Capacity Manager should talk to:

* the customers and to Customer Liaison personnel, to elicit:
    - their view of the service which is currently provided by IT
    - presence (or absence) of business forecasts
    - work patterns including peak periods
    - workforce changes
    - known business growth/decline
    - planned changes, eg number of terminals/ workstations, changes of functionality, workforce and so on
    - service availability needs, present and future
* the IT Director, to discover his views about:
    - the IT Directorate's own business objectives (is it a profit or cost centre)
    - availability of IT and user business plans for use in capacity management
    - the importance of customer service
    - the perceived role of capacity management within the organization
    - the information requirements from capacity management
    - details of any proposed changes, typically items which cut across business applications, eg use of office systems or decision support tools, new technology and so on

* the IT Services Manager, to ascertain views on:
  - the quality of the service that is currently provided to the users
  - effectiveness of communication, both with users and within IT especially in respect to performance and capacity issues
  - currently perceived problem areas
  - organizational issues with respect to capacity management (ie where it should be positioned)
* the Application Development Manager, to determine:
  - the effectiveness of communication with IT Services
  - the effectiveness of communication with users
  - the role of service levels within the development lifecycle, ie are they part of the deliverables for each completed application
  - any requirement to change system design standards to include application sizing as an integral part of the development lifecycle and to provide the necessary data to allow capacity management to take place
* the Service Level Manager and the Availability Manager, to ascertain the current scope of service levels within the organization; in particular:
  - distribution of computer capacity to facilitate availability and resilience
  - use of resource intensive 4GLs
  - whether service level agreements exist, and if so what they specify
  - whether the current levels of service are meeting existing service level agreements, or if none exist then whether user requirements are being met
  - what major application changes are planned (new systems coming on-stream, old ones being phased out)
  - any constraints affecting service delivery
  - customer response

* the Network Manager, to obtain a total view of the organization's telecommunications infrastructure and to gain commitment to the implementation of capacity management for the data network.
* the Cost Manager to gain an awareness of the current scope of cost management, the requirements for data from capacity management and details of the budget cycle
* the Computer Operations Manager to establish a view on the service which is provided to the users and any constraints which may affect the delivery of that service
* the Performance Manager (if separated from the Capacity Manager) to discover the scope, content and frequency of
    - any existing performance monitoring or tuning
    - details of existing monitors and tools.

Discussions should take place with any additional personnel who can usefully contribute to the understanding of the current state of the organization. Ensure that there are adequate lines of communication especially between performance, capacity and service management personnel.

3.1.6 Produce project plan

The Capacity Manager should now assess the results of the meetings and investigations and produce a project plan.

A detailed project plan should be created that describes the introduction or improvement of the capacity management function.

The project plan should detail:

* activities and dependencies
* end products
* required resources
* timescales
* costs
* organization
* controls
* risks.

The activities and their end-products should be based on the information obtained from the steps defined in the detailed review and the gap analysis. The activities could address the following issues:

* staff issues, such as organization structure, recruitment and training
* tool selection, procurement, installation, adaptation, testing
* mounting an awareness campaign
* testing of procedures, tools, support systems and documentation
* accommodation and environmental requirements
* establishment of implementation procedures.

It is important to specify in the project plan that capacity management is best implemented in stages.

The detailed project plan must be formally approved by the Project Board.

Capacity management can take a long time to implement fully. Therefore, the Capacity Manager should make every effort to produce early deliverables, otherwise impatience is likely to ensue, followed by lack of interest. Section 4.1.9 provides some ideas for an initial implementation plan.

The project plan may be constrained by the lack of human resources or the need to produce early deliverables. In this situation consider the use of contractors and/or consultants, if funds are available. One advantage of this approach is the ready availability of expertise in capacity management which could be passed on to the capacity management team.

Sections 3.1.6.1-3.1.6.7 define in more detail the main prerequisites for production of a capacity plan (production of a capacity plan is covered in section 3.1.6.8). Sections 3.1.6.9 and 3.1.6.10 outline the essential interfaces (to service management and to cost management) that should be reviewed each time a capacity plan is produced. References to more detailed descriptions of the main tasks are given throughout this guidance. The detailed information can be referenced if the Capacity Manager wishes to expand this skeleton data.

3.1.6.1 Software review

This review is necessary if it was not completed during the initial study - see also Annex B.

Objectives

* ensure that sufficient tools are available to collect data
* assess the suitability of current tools

Main tasks

* check that tools can provide the data which is necessary for capacity management
* evaluate modelling tools - guidance is given on this subject in section 7
* establish requirements for any specific reporting tools, graphics, word processing, desk top publishing etc.

Deliverables

* justification for purchase of any additional tools which are considered to be required for capacity management. Such justification should centre upon the requirement for better management control of capacity and performance which is essential for the effective provision of quality IT services.

3.1.6.2 Performance management

See Annex C for further information about performance management.

Objectives

* ensure that agreed service levels are maintained
* ensure that optimum use is made of all hardware and software resources.

Main tasks

* monitor the system on a daily basis
* identify and recommend rectification of instances of substandard performance
* ensure that releases of new systems software do not cause a deterioration in performance

* performance assessment of new hardware
* taking the lead role in all tuning exercises
* ensure that all required technical data is stored in the CDB in the appropriate detailed or summarized form - see 3.1.6.3.

Deliverables

* provision of a service which makes optimum use of the hardware and software resources and gives early warning when service levels are in danger of not being maintained, and when other thresholds (indicating that capacity is at a premium or is being used inefficiently) may be exceeded.

3.1.6.3 Capacity Management Database (CDB)

Conceptually, a single database containing all the information relevant to capacity and configuration management is needed. Few organizations can afford the time, the money or the hardware to realize the concept of a single database. The CDB guidance throughout this module is written to reflect the ideal concept of a single database, which in the future may be a practical proposition. Aim to make the CDB the central repository for capacity management information. See also Annex C.

Objectives

* design, size, build and maintain a database which contains all technical, business and cost data that is required by capacity management
* produce technical and management reports which show current usage and trends.

Main tasks

* design CDB with due regard to the amount of detailed and summary level technical data which must be stored
* decide on all other items of data to be kept in the database, eg business objectives, service level objectives, hardware thresholds, costing information
* create/maintain CDB
* design a standard set of management reports covering the current week/month and trends; also design exception reports

* document contents of CDB, operating procedures and recovery actions.

Deliverables

* CDB the contents of which are appropriate to the capacity management function
* a standard set of management reports covering the current period and previous historical trends
* operating procedures for the building and maintenance of the CDB plus details of the frequency and distribution of the reports.

3.1.6.4 Workload management

Workload management is given more detailed coverage in Annex D.

Objectives

* understand and document all workloads
* establish effective and formal interfaces to relevant parties, within IT (and external to IT) for the interchange of information
* implement an effective workload forecasting system.

Main tasks

* identify, understand and document workloads; in particular, understand working patterns and peaks of individual systems in terms of their resource requirements
* publish and maintain a workload catalogue
* produce and maintain resource profiles for major transactions/jobs
* perform regular workload forecasting exercises, typically once per quarter.

Deliverables

* workload catalogue
* workload forecasting system
* quarterly workload forecasting report.

3.1.6.5 Modelling

Modelling is a particularly important technique for the Capacity Manager. More detailed information is supplied in Annex E.

Objectives

* ensure availability of appropriate tools
* produce a model of the current system which has been calibrated against actual workload data, and is accurate within 5-10% of actual loadings

Main tasks

The main tasks depend to a large extent on the type of modelling tool available. Some essential tasks are mentioned below:

* understand the workloads
* extract data as appropriate from system monitors, audit logs and accounting journals
* utilize modelling facilities to produce baseline model
* calibrate the model (eg apportionment of filestore transfers to individual discs in the model).

Deliverables

* individual models of workloads
* calibrated baseline model of overall workload.

3.1.6.6 Sizing of new applications

Refer to Annexes F and J for additional information, and to the CCTA Subject Guide describing **SSADM V4 and Capacity Planning**.

Objectives

* establish mechanisms to predict the service level resource and cost implications of any new application or any major addition to an existing application.

Main tasks

* look at development methodology standards to ensure that the information which is required by capacity management is available at each stage of the development lifecycle

* establish sizing as an **integral** part of the development lifecycle
* develop sizing methodology and evaluate the use of tools to assist this process
* identify options to improve or degrade service levels and assess the cost of these options
* establish mechanisms for feeding back the results of sizing exercises to the project team; eg expected levels of service, identification of likely performance bottlenecks, and cost implications.

Deliverables

* development standards which take note of service level implications, in addition to issues of functionality
* sizing reports which are produced at all stages of the lifecycle to provide essential information on estimated service level and cost implications.

3.1.6.7 Resource management

Resource management should include liaison with both the availability and configuration managers. The IT Infrastructure Library guides on **Availability Management** and **Configuration Management** should be referenced.

Objectives

* understand the organization's hardware, software, infrastructure and other resources
* produce a hardware updating plan
* understand and document the vulnerabilities of the service (to performance bottlenecks)
* ensure that the organization is aware of any changes in technology (speedier disc access, etc) with the concomitant impacts on performance and cost.

Main tasks

* identify when to purchase new hardware and software
* maintain accurate configuration diagrams with the assistance of the configuration management team
* document the resource needs of the organization as a schedule of resources

* define a storage management system (if appropriate)
* establish interfaces with manufacturers, third-party vendors, user groups etc to ensure that the latest information is available on new technology announcements
* assess the possible benefits of new technology to the organization.

Deliverables

* a schedule which details resources available to the IT Services Manager (hardware, software, infrastructure resources, storage, business and resilience requirements and configuration plans). See also resource profiles (workload management - Annex D.3)
* up-to-date configuration diagrams
* evaluation reports of the impact of new technology on the organization in terms of performance/cost benefits.
* storage management system.

3.1.6.8 Production of the capacity plan

Objectives

* produce a capacity plan at agreed intervals which fit into the business planning cycle, eg the financial year.

Main tasks

* establish mechanisms for the collection of business planning data
* identify the level of management approval for agreeing the scope of the plan
* calculate the effects on service levels and hardware utilizations of the estimated demand over the period of the planning horizon
* produce a capacity plan which shows the effects of changes in service levels, (eg impact on capacity, any recommendations for upgrading/ downgrading of hardware, accommodating or suppressing demand and the associated costs)

* agree the capacity plan and its implications with IT management (viz, more hardware, improved or degraded service levels or revised workloads).

Deliverable

* the capacity plan (see section 4.1.6).

3.1.6.9 Interface to service level management

Objectives

* provide information to the Service Level Manager on estimated levels of service which can be achieved and maintained for existing systems
* calculate likely service levels for new applications
* discuss the hardware necessary to meet different service level options.

Main tasks

* decide with the Service Level Manager which components of the service can be monitored automatically and conversely, which items would have to be monitored manually
* assess the need for demand management (section 5.1.8); if the systems regularly exhibit capacity problems, the Capacity Manager must plan for managing excess demands
* design, agree with the Service Level Manager and implement a service level monitoring system which is appropriate for the organization
* produce reports daily with weekly/monthly summaries
* create a mechanism whereby the Service Level Manager can be supplied with estimated service levels to assist in negotiations with the users (this will probably include the need for modelling tools).

Deliverables

* estimates on future service levels
* service level monitoring reporting system.

3.1.6.10 Interface to cost management

Note here that for network capacity management, circuit costing is sometimes a task carried out by the Network Capacity Planner, rather than the Cost Manager. This is because trading-off circuit costs against performance is usually a prime task of the Network Capacity Planner.

Objectives

* provide the Cost Manager with sufficient information about hardware and software costs and usage to allow formulation and implementation of an equitable cost recovery strategy and expenditure management
* ensure that adequate job accounting data is maintained to allow costs to be broken down by business usage and to facilitate the implementation of a fair chargeback system where required.

Main task

* liaise with the Cost Manager to agree the requirement for information on past, present and estimated future usage of hardware resources, overall and by workload.

Deliverable

* provision of data which leads to satisfactory cost management.

3.1.6.11 Awareness campaign

The success of capacity management depends upon the commitment of all parties, in particular, customers, senior management, and IT Services personnel. It is essential that everyone is made aware of the reasons why capacity management is being introduced and the benefits to the entire organization and to them personally.

The most effective method of communicating this message is by means of formal presentations which address:

* capacity
    - explaining what is capacity management ie: matching demand to hardware resources to provide appropriate levels of service (a brief description of the component parts of capacity management, as detailed in section 2.3.1 could be provided)

  - prerequisites for successful capacity management, such as commitment from all participants, especially senior management, that capacity management is part of an overall strategy and management process. Note: It should be emphasized that capacity management is a continuous process and cannot be done as a one-off exercise or even a series of one-off exercises; and it will not be implemented or delivered overnight.

* strategies
  - the need to cope with, for example changing environments, the introduction of fourth generation programming languages (4GLs), relational databases and new hardware
  - providing a quality service
  - ensuring organizational financial stability
  - ensuring there are no sudden, unforeseen demands for major upgrades.
* performance
  - optimum economic and efficient use of resources
  - implementation of cost-effective systems
  - emphasis on effective planning rather than continually reacting to crises
  - the implementation and ongoing operation plan: when deliverables will be produced after implementation and how often thereafter.

Ensure that written backup material is provided (copies of slides, reports and so on) to supplement the presentations.

3.1.7 Roles, responsibilities and staff requirements

The role and responsibilities of the Capacity Manager are discussed in 3.1.1.

This section deals with the overall responsibilities of the team.

An adequately staffed capacity management team is necessary to:

* produce and maintain the capacity plan
* monitor service levels
* recommend tuning
* manage demand
* recommend capacity enhancements
* account for changes in the workload or in service level targets.

The team needs skilled, properly trained personnel, with a sound understanding of system architecture, standards and of the way in which work flows through the network, the operating system, the TP monitor, database and file-handling software. The team may wish to get additional help from consultants, but the team itself **must** be skilled. Capacity management can only be effective in competent hands.

The capacity management team needs to have an understanding of the organization's business. It should be staffed by people who can relate to managers and users at all levels in order to obtain information on business and strategic plans.

Permanence

The team should be permanently staffed: capacity management should be a continuous process, and not just an isolated, or series of isolated, sizing or tuning exercises. Even where the organization's workload is stable, staff is required, independent of your operations staff, to monitor service quality continuously and to translate business plans to IT capacity plans.

Training

All staff must be fully trained in the use of support tools and procedures. It is essential to create a training plan which can be used to schedule appropriate training for each of the individuals in the capacity management team. This training plan would ensure that the work does not suffer at the expense of training and vice versa.

Customers need to be educated about business capacity and performance issues both for the planning of new applications and for the optimization of existing ones. The capacity management team should be responsible for these activities. The capacity management team may need from time to time to explain to users their recommendations on demand management.

3.1.8 Select support tools

Using the guidance provided in section 7 and in the Annexes (particularly Annex B) the support tools should be chosen. In general it is not advisable to attempt sizing (or modelling) without the use of a software tool, although there are individuals who are trained in the methods of hand-sizing. In general, hand-sizing will produce results comparable with software: unfortunately it takes many years to become an expert in hand-sizing.

Similarly, modelling tools are now virtually indispensable because of the speed with which they can produce reasonably accurate results.

Fundamentally, you must choose tools which will enhance or facilitate capacity management functions. The choice may be determined by the content of the framework description (3.1.4) or simply on the basis of compatibility with other tools.

The selection of tools will, however, usually comprise:

* sampling/monitoring tool
* data manipulation/graphics tool
* modelling/sizing tool
* perhaps a word processor and/or a spreadsheet.

3.1.9 Accommodation and environment

Factors to be considered should be:

* proximity to related functions (eg SLM, configuration management)
* separation of capacity planning from day-to-day performance management responsibilities (see also 3.3.2).

3.2 Dependencies

The primary dependence is commitment from all parties (users, senior management, IT management and IT personnel). Their commitment will undoubtedly depend on the success of the awareness campaign and its ability to convince people of the benefits to the organization as a whole and to them in particular.

The jigsaw

The variety of functions described in the IT Infrastructure Library makes it difficult to identify what should be implemented first, and what should be the general order of implementation. It is recommended that the functions are implemented broadly in accordance with the jigsaw diagram (Figure 2). However, as with all jigsaws it is the overall result that matters: there are many different solutions to the problem; some solutions are more efficient than others.

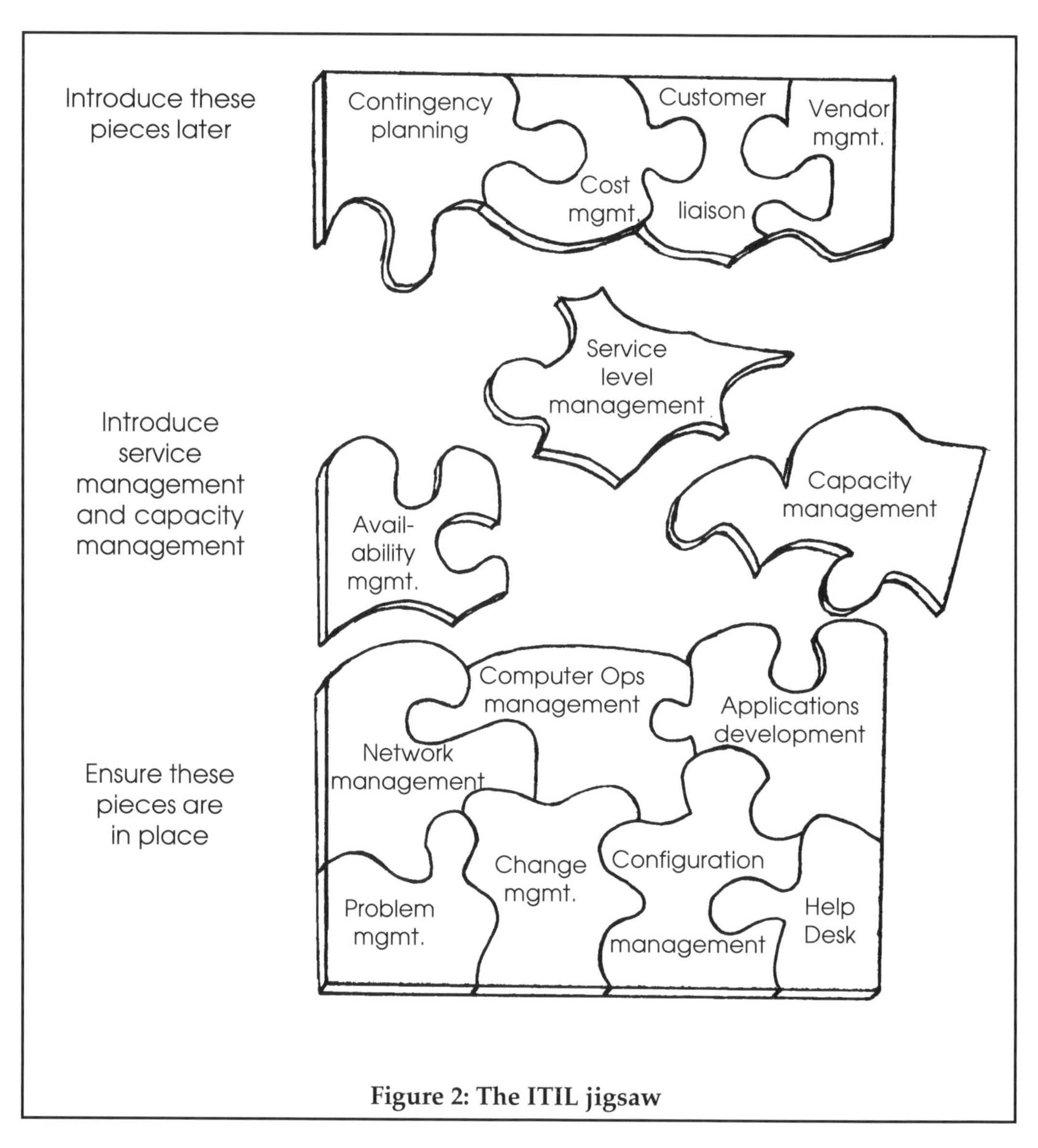

Figure 2: The ITIL jigsaw

There are no functional dependencies which will prevent the implementation of capacity management. As mentioned earlier it is preferable, though not essential, that the supporting processes are established (if they do not already exist). The most important element is change management since the capacity plans should be subject to that process. Service level management should, of course, be established as soon as possible since the provision of a quality service is the principal aim of capacity management.

Finally, ensure that the required tools will be available for monitoring, data manipulation, reporting and modelling.

3.3 People

3.3.1 Capacity Manager

The Capacity Manager has responsibility for ensuring that IT Services management is correctly advised on how to:

* match capacity and demand by increasing or managing available capacity
* ensure that existing capacity is used in an optimum manner.

The Capacity Manager is also responsible for advising the Service Level Manager about appropriate service levels or service level options. The ideal background for a Capacity Manager is therefore a person who has been involved in applications development, IT services provision and data communications: in short, the ultimate generalist. However, such individuals are difficult to find. It is therefore usual to find Capacity Managers recruited from either the application development or computer services area. Consider staff for the post who:

* have good interpersonal skills and can relate to managers and customers at all levels
* understand the organization's business
* communicate well orally and in writing
* comprehend the concepts of hardware, operating software and networks.

If a separate Network Capacity Manager is to be appointed it should normally be a computer literate person with extensive telecommunications experience or a telecommunications person with extensive computer experience. The job has a high technical and analytical content and may require management of a small team of technical specialists. To this extent, the qualifications and experience required are similar to those of a computer systems-programming team leader. Indeed, this may be seen as a career move for network systems programmers or for particularly able network operations personnel.

It is difficult to be precise, but an installation which has 100 or more IT staff would normally justify a full-time Computer Capacity Manager. For the network, a user population of 200 or more terminals would justify a full-time Network Capacity Manager. Several part-time staff may be a viable alternative if they have complementary skills. However, be aware that the use of several part-time staff may lead to clashes of availability and subsequent delays in the completion of tasks. The part-time approach is therefore not recommended unless circumstances dictate otherwise.

3.3.2 Capacity management section

The capacity management function has many facets, but two in particular are generally considered to be of particular value: performance monitoring and capacity planning. In organizations which can justify more than one full- or part-time person, the duties should be split into monitoring/tuning and planning, because staff who are involved in day-to-day monitoring and tuning activities tend to have difficulty in standing back from crises and seeing planning from a dispassionate viewpoint.

The person(s) responsible for monitoring and tuning activities should preferably have had previous experience of such tasks as a systems programmer or computer operations support person. Recruitment of computer capacity planning staff should be from either applications development (systems analysis) or elsewhere in IT Services management; a background in both is preferable. For network capacity planning, a background in telecommunications and/or data networks operations is appropriate.

In large organizations extra staff will be required, though it is difficult to be precise on staffing numbers. For host capacity management the size will depend upon the amount of hardware and the volatility of applications. For organizations with a single CPU system, one person devoted to performance/tuning and one person devoted to planning should typically be adequate. However, the planning team, in organizations where there is a great deal of development, may have one or more people whose sole task is to size new or amended applications. Organizations which have multiple computer systems or multiple locations may well require additional staff.

On the network side much depends upon the complexity and rate of change of the network or networks. However, a network based upon a high-speed backbone, such as one consisting of large packet switches linked by Megastream circuits, with low-speed feeder sub-networks will have two levels of capacity management: one related to bandwidth provision and packet switch performance, the other to applications data transmission considerations. This may entail the use of two staff. For the very largest networks (ie those with tens of thousands of terminals), the monitoring and planning aspects may also be split, implying a total of four staff reporting to the Network Capacity Manager.

Smaller organizations may be able to justify only part-time staff. It is possible but highly unlikely (because of their different technical backgrounds) that computer and network capacity planning could be carried out by a single person in a small installation; two part-time staff would make a more effective solution. It is worth investigating how much assistance the Telecommunications Manager can give in staffing resource for Network capacity management. If staff resources are unavailable, it will be necessary to tailor the scope of the capacity management system which is detailed in this module.

Because the majority of organizations perceive capacity management as a mainframe-oriented activity, this guidance has been collated fundamentally as a mainframe/ network reference work. It is recognized that part-time Capacity Managers, sites using distributed systems or microcomputers and the installation of computer systems on greenfield sites each has particular characteristics. With this in mind, a number of annexes have been provided in this module which include additional information specific to these particular subjects. The information can be found in:

* Annex G - part-time capacity management
* Annex H - distributed systems
* Annex I - different software platforms
* Annex J - greenfield sites
* Annex K - microcomputers.

3.3.3 Other liaisons

Figure 2 (page 36) illustrates the principal liaisons with other parts of the organization.

3.3.4 Placement in the organization

The level of responsibility which is accorded to capacity management is determined largely by its positioning within the organization. Capacity management requires a high profile if its importance is to be recognized by senior management. The preferred positioning is as a part of the IT Directorate's Service Management group. Unfortunately, there is a natural tendency in many organizations to site it within Computer Operations. This is not an ideal position since users and application development staff may well take the view that any judgements which are made by capacity management staff are likely to reflect only the wishes of Computer Operations.

Take care when determining where the network capacity management function will reside within the management structure. It should be within the IT Directorate if that organization includes telecommunications services within its ambit. However, difficulties may arise where telephone services are the responsibility of another Directorate. These difficulties may be avoided if note is taken of the following points.

Network capacity management requires a blend of telecommunications and computer skills. Where Telecommunications and Data Processing Departments are separate, locate the network capacity management function in the IT Directorate because the amount of liaison required with staff and users is usually somewhat greater than that required with telecommunications staff. However, staff to carry out this function are likely to be recruited from both departments, because of the skill requirements.

Network management and configuration management

It is usual for the Network Manager to have a Configuration Database which holds details of the locations of all network equipment. The maintenance of this database is largely a clerical, administrative function. Capacity management of the network implies keeping data in parallel to that held in the Configuration Management Database(CMDB) relating to the performance and utilization of the network equipment. Maintenance of the network capacity management data is usually carried out either by Network

Operations or by the Network Capacity Manager. It is possible but not desirable to keep these two sets of information as two separate databases; they must be linked to avoid planning and management inconsistencies.

Because of the complex technical nature and relationships of the various items of data, whether held in such an integrated database (referred to as the Network Database elsewhere in this module) or in separate databases, a higher level of technical competence is required than would normally be expected of a clerical administrator. The qualifications and experience required for this overall custodian of the network data are those normally found in a systems analyst; in general, the bigger the database, the higher are the qualifications required. Thus there might be difficulties in placing a person of this seniority into the standard Network Administration function. It is therefore recommended that a Network Database custodian is appointed to report directly to the Network Manager.

3.3.5 Training

Complement the existing skills of the capacity management team by suitable additional training.

Training courses based on the Service Delivery and Service Support sets of the IT Infrastructure Library (ITIL) are available, leading to the award of a certificate of proficiency. The certificate may be enhanced at a later date when other courses are available on the remaining ITIL sets.

External courses, three to five days in duration, are available which provide a comprehensive introduction to the subject. In addition, courses on individual subjects within capacity management, eg workload forecasting, application sizing or resource management are available. They typically last three or four days.

Send staff who require skills in the area of performance monitoring and tuning on courses about the operating software (which are run by the hardware/software vendors). Such courses are typically one to two weeks in duration.

Training in the use of modelling tools which have been purchased may also be required. Negotiate any training requirements with the vendor before purchase. Courses which cover the modelling methodology for a single hardware/software platform will typically last two or three days.

Consider training in the areas of report writing, public speaking and inter-personal skills for individual staff members, where this is appropriate.

3.4 Timing

It is best to align the introduction of capacity management with the beginning of a new financial year. There are interfaces with other functions, as stated in section 2.4, and it would be better if those areas were already in existence but their absence should not prevent the commencement of capacity management. However, it is strongly recommended that configuration, change and problem management functions **are** in place.

Service level management and cost management should be implemented to follow capacity management or as soon after as possible. The interfaces to these areas should be defined when they are required.

Network Capacity Planning should be in place at the planning stage of the first phase of the network since it is vital to the cost-effective provision of circuits. Service level management relies on its results and the Network Database is one of its essential tools.

The amount of time which is taken to complete the planning stage of capacity management will depend upon the size and complexity of the installation plus the experience of the people involved. However, it is considered that both host and network planning studies will each take in the region of 6-8 person weeks for an installation with around 100 IT staff.

4. Implementation

4.1 Procedures

The majority of the tasks which must be addressed by capacity management are performed regularly. This section provides guidance on the initial implementation of the aspects of capacity management. Where necessary, each major topic is split up into host and network elements. The host element is applicable to mainframe and minicomputer installations: Annex J gives guidance on micro-based systems. The network element is applicable to both wide area networks (WANs) and local area networks (LANs).

Guidance is given on the order in which to tackle individual tasks with the emphasis on getting a basic system in place as soon as possible, and thus producing early deliverables.

4.1.1 Implement performance management

One of the first tasks is to establish the performance management function.

The objective of implementing performance management is to ensure that optimum use is made of the hardware and software resources in order that agreed service levels can be maintained. The key to successful performance management is to pre-empt problems wherever possible; ie the process should be anticipatory, rather than reactive.

There are two main elements of performance management: monitoring current performance, and improving it by tuning (see figure 3, overleaf). Annex C provides detailed information about these performance issues and also covers the use of exception reporting.

4.1.2 CDB and reporting system

This sub-section is particularly concerned with how the information held in a CDB is used in the production of reports. Figure 4, overleaf, illustrates the major processes which feed in to the database and which are the raw material for the reports. More detailed guidance about implementing a CDB is provided in Annex C.

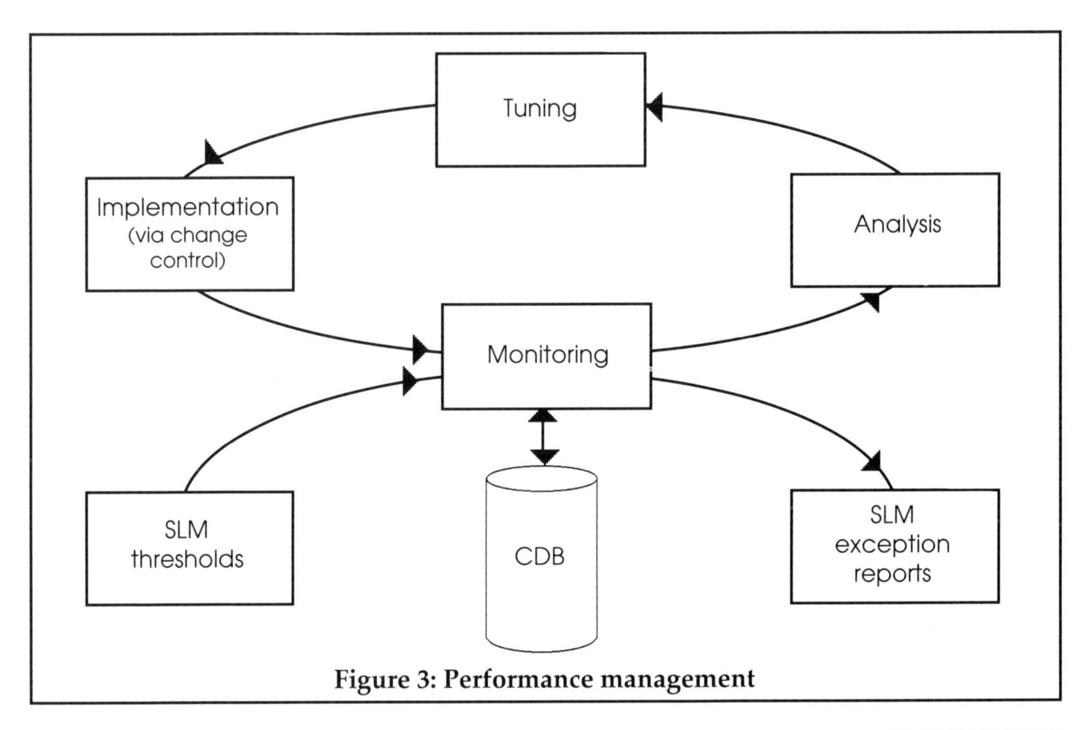

Figure 3: Performance management

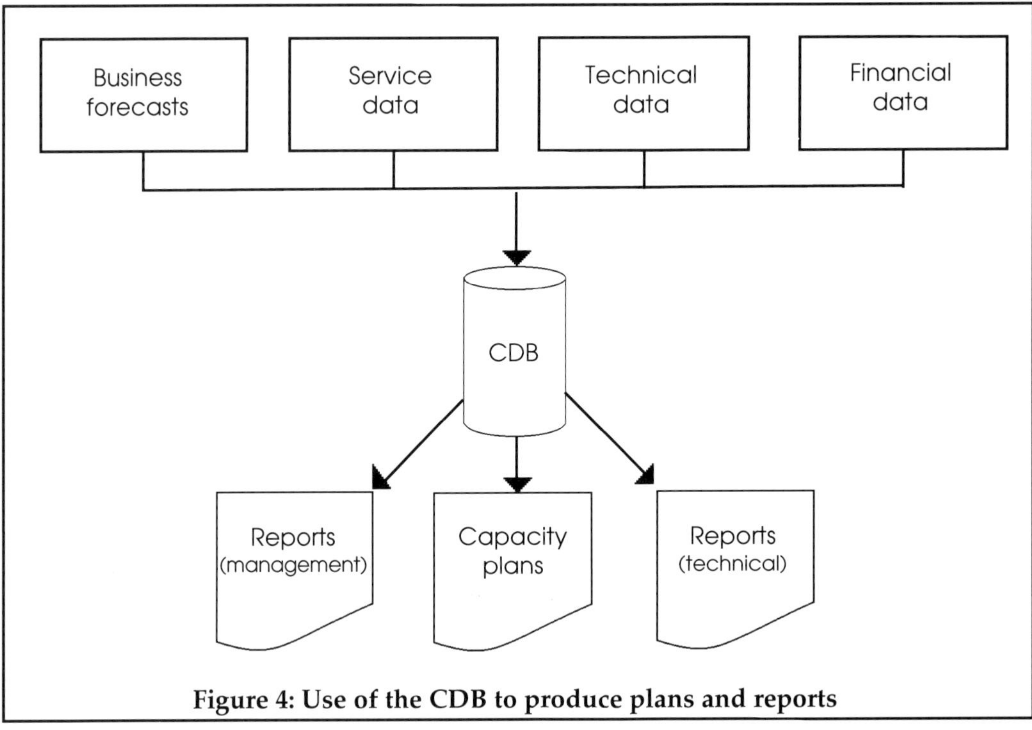

Figure 4: Use of the CDB to produce plans and reports

4.1.3 Plans and reports

The Capacity Manager will be expected to produce both plans and reports. The plans and reports fall into three categories.

Firstly, there are capacity plans. Pay particular attention to consistency of approach and terminology when preparing capacity plans for host and network.

Secondly, there are regular management reports. These should show usage trends relating to each Service Level Agreement (SLA), giving advance warning of insufficient capacity and the changes required to deal with it. Additional information should be provided as the need arises if there is an unexpected change in capacity demand, a problem frequently caused by network traffic not covered by SLAs. These reports should be produced monthly.

Finally, there are technical reports, ie answers to specific questions, such as determining the best upgrade path to take to improve performance for a specific user. These take the form of short reports containing results of analysis of current performance data and model results, and are technical in nature. These reports are produced as and when required.

Some examples of the style of reports that can be produced are in Annex L.

4.1.4 Implement workload management

Figure 5, overleaf, illustrates the role of workload management in the capacity management function.

Workload management is crucial to capacity management. The data used to practice workload management tends to be accumulated over fairly lengthy periods. Identifying trends, for example, is difficult without large volumes of statistics (this is true whether it is desired to identify a daily, weekly or monthly trend). This sub-section is therefore included as a guide to the processes. Annex D, Workload Management, describes each of the main tasks in detail.

The primary objective of workload management is to produce a set of forecasts which will indicate estimated resource usage up to the agreed planning horizon: eg two years. However, there are a number of prerequisites before a forecasting exercise can be attempted.

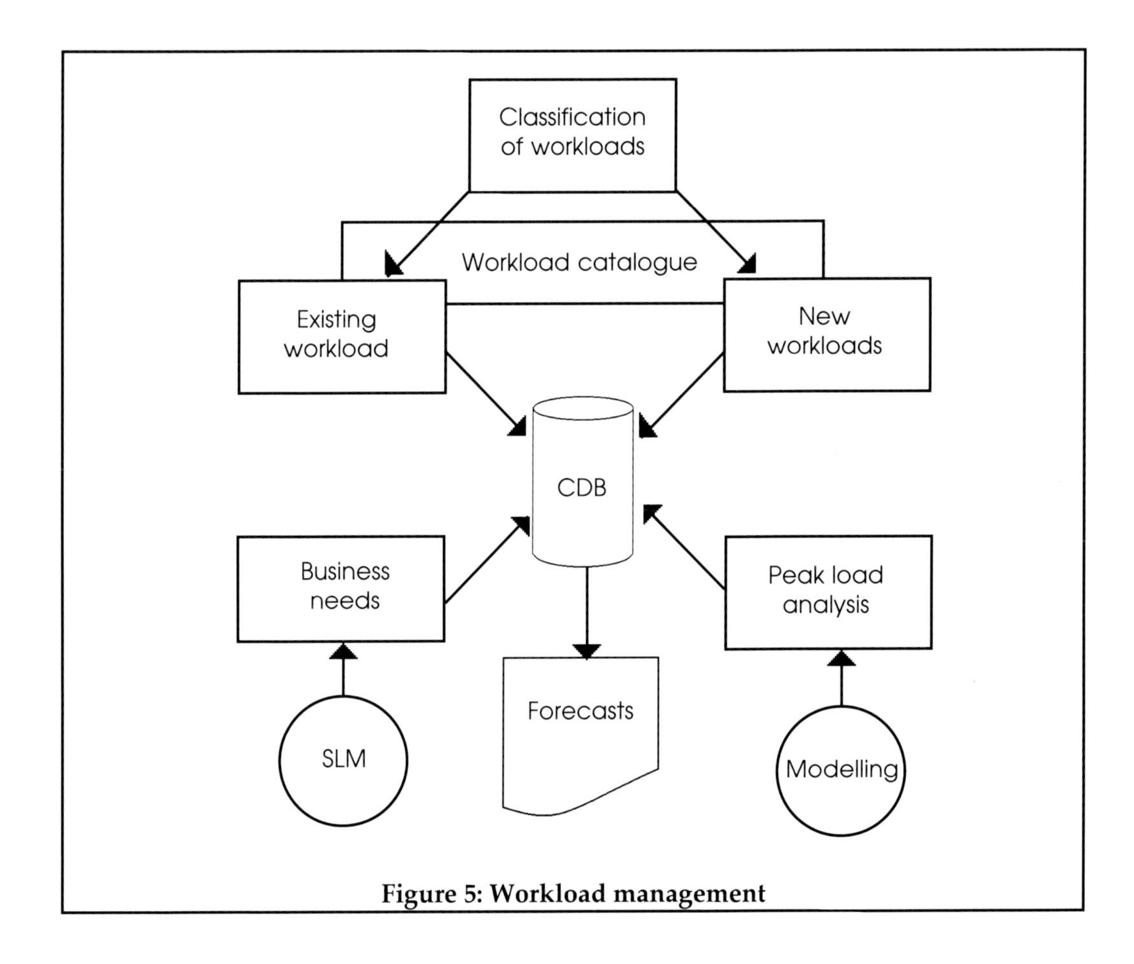

Figure 5: Workload management

A clear understanding must be obtained of the workloads which run on the hardware, the resources consumed and when the resources are used. The time period of planning concern must be identified, eg the peak hour of the average day, or peak day at the end of the month.

4.1.5 Resource management

This sub-section contains details of a number of discrete, ancillary tasks which are grouped together under the title of resource management (see figure 6). Tasks undertaken by workload management are sometimes classified as resource management and it is recommended that Annex D (particularly D.3, Resource Profiles) is consulted so that the demarcation lines drawn by this particular module are clear.

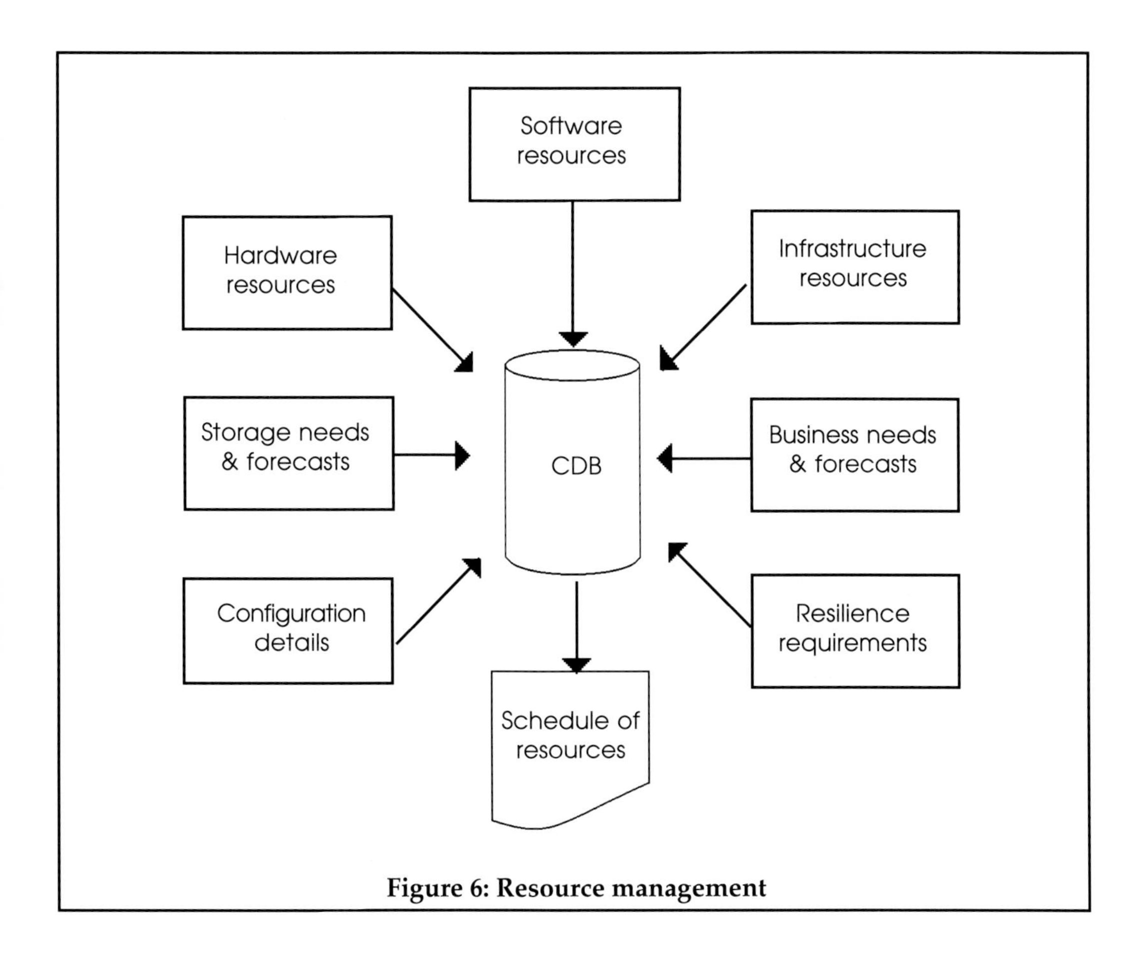

Figure 6: Resource management

Configuration diagram

The production and maintenance of accurate host configuration diagrams should be the responsibility of the Capacity Manager. Close liaison with the Configuration Manager is necessary to accomplish this task. Some manufacturers charge their engineers with the task of producing up-to-date configuration diagrams.

Distribute copies to the Configuration Manager and other interested parties.

Schedule of resources

From the Configuration Manager, obtain a schedule of the resources available to the IT Services teams including hardware, software and infrastructure resources. The requirements of the business (ie the workloads), resilience, storage and the configuration plans mentioned above should be included. Distribute copies as appropriate: the information will be needed for the capacity plan.

Resilience

In organizations practising availability management, resilience is often the responsibility of both the Capacity Manager and the Availability Manager. Together they must establish how vulnerable the hardware and software platforms are to failure of individual components and make recommendations on any cost effective solutions. For example, multiple paths to the application database provide protection against the failure of a single channel or controller.

Understand how susceptible the current configuration is to failure. Component Failure Impact Analysis (CFIA) is a simple but useful technique, introduced by IBM, which can help to highlight any potential problems for each workload. A matrix is drawn which shows, in order of their importance, the system components as columns and the applications as rows. An example is shown in Figure 7.

Group description	Software					Hardware					
Item Number	1	2	3	4	5	6	7	8	9	10	11
Component	OP Sys	TP Mon	DBMS	timeshr	Environ	CPU	console	DCU #1	DCU #2	DCU #3	disks
Number available	-	-	-	-	-	2	1	1	1	1	40
Applications											
Operating software	X	-	-	-	X	A	-	X	-	-	6
Accounting	X	X	X	-	X	A	A	X	A	A	17
Personnel	X	X	-	-	X	A	A	X	A	A	8
Decision support	X	-	-	X	X	A	X	X	-	X	4
E-mail	X	-	-	-	X	A	X	X	-	X	3
Development	X	-	-	X	X	A	X	X	-	X	-
Procedure number	1	3	2	4	5	7	6	8	8	8	9

Key:

X failure of a component causes the loss of service for that workload.

A there is an alternative device

F there is an alternative path } *Not used in*

B there is a backup device } *this example*

digit minimum number of devices of that type required to run the application.

Figure 7: CFIA grid

Each application is investigated to gain information to complete the grid. If this process is carried out in a comprehensive manner then the Capacity Manager or Availability Manager probably needs to produce supplementary material to provide the detail behind the grid. For example, an expansion worksheet may be produced for each system component (identified by the item number) which gives the following detail for each system component/application cell on the grid:

* the problem(s)
* any bypass/recovery action
* the overall effect caused by the problem
* any issues/needs or recommendations.

Use the results of the investigative work as the foundation for 'what if?' analyses to investigate the possible benefits and cost-effectiveness of additional hardware where this may be appropriate. The use of a modelling tool can facilitate this work. Examples of areas which can be analyzed include:

* use of fault tolerant hardware where this is appropriate
* multiple CPUs
* independent banks of memory
* multiple paths to the disk/tape devices via controllers and channels
* mirroring of disks
* duplex journalling.

A further byproduct of CFIA may be to produce a set of procedures, if they do not already exist, which specify the bypass or recovery procedures. The compilation of such procedures should be carried out by Computer Operations.

Storage management

In many IT installations this task is not part of capacity management. It is usually carried out within computer operations support or technical support. If this is the case, and there is effective liaison with capacity management, there is no reason to move it.

The main tasks of storage management are to:

* be responsible for the allocation of disk space
* ensure optimum disk usage by allocation of the appropriate amount of space (this can be done by validating all requests for large amounts of disk space; eg if more than 5% of total available space is required)
* ensure that satisfactory naming conventions are employed so that the owners of the disk space can be identified
* ensure optimum usage of disk space by the regular deletion or archiving of unwanted or unused data
* forecast future requirements, as part of workload forecasting and application sizing
* produce reports on current and planned disk usage.

External interfaces

It is imperative that the Capacity Manager establishes contacts with external organizations to improve the effectiveness of the function. In particular, contacts should be encouraged with:

* hardware and software vendors to be aware of, understand and make optimum usage of the current hardware and software products and changes in technology
* users of similar hardware and products, to increase the dissemination of useful knowledge
* for example, UKCMG, the user group specifically for capacity management. (At least one member of the organization chould be a member of UKCMG and attend the annual conference and any appropriate sub-group sessions which are held throughout the year).

New technology and changes

The Capacity Manager should ensure that the organization is aware of all relevant changes in technology. Assess such changes to establish their significance to the organization in terms of increased performance and cost-effectiveness.

Examples of possible changes based on new technology may include:

* faster CPUs
* faster channels
* cache controllers
* faster disk or tape controllers
* disks with greater capacity
* parallel processing architectures
* solid state devices
* optical disks
* use of hypervisors or other firmware facilities which allow multiple operating systems to co-exist in one machine
* effects of mirroring/duplexing on performance.

Other changes which should be assessed include:

* use of multiple CPUs
* increased memory
* use of more controllers.

4.1.6 Production of capacity plan

The processes leading to production of the capacity plan are represented in figure 8, overleaf. The objective is to use current sets of workload forecasts to produce a capacity plan which details the estimated hardware requirements needed to meet the agreed service levels for the next twelve months. The plan should also outline the requirements for the subsequent year(s).

Produce a capacity plan before the annual budget planning cycle commences so that it can provide the necessary input. Produce quarterly updates of the plan to be used predominantly as a means of checking the validity of the original plan, and of providing forward notice of any unexpected developments.

Plan the scenario

It is important that the scenario, on which the plan is based, is agreed by the IT Director, the IT Services Manager and the Service Level Manager. It is quite common to produce a plan after a lot of work, only to discover that the results (usually the expenditure implications) are rejected and the plan has to be reworked.

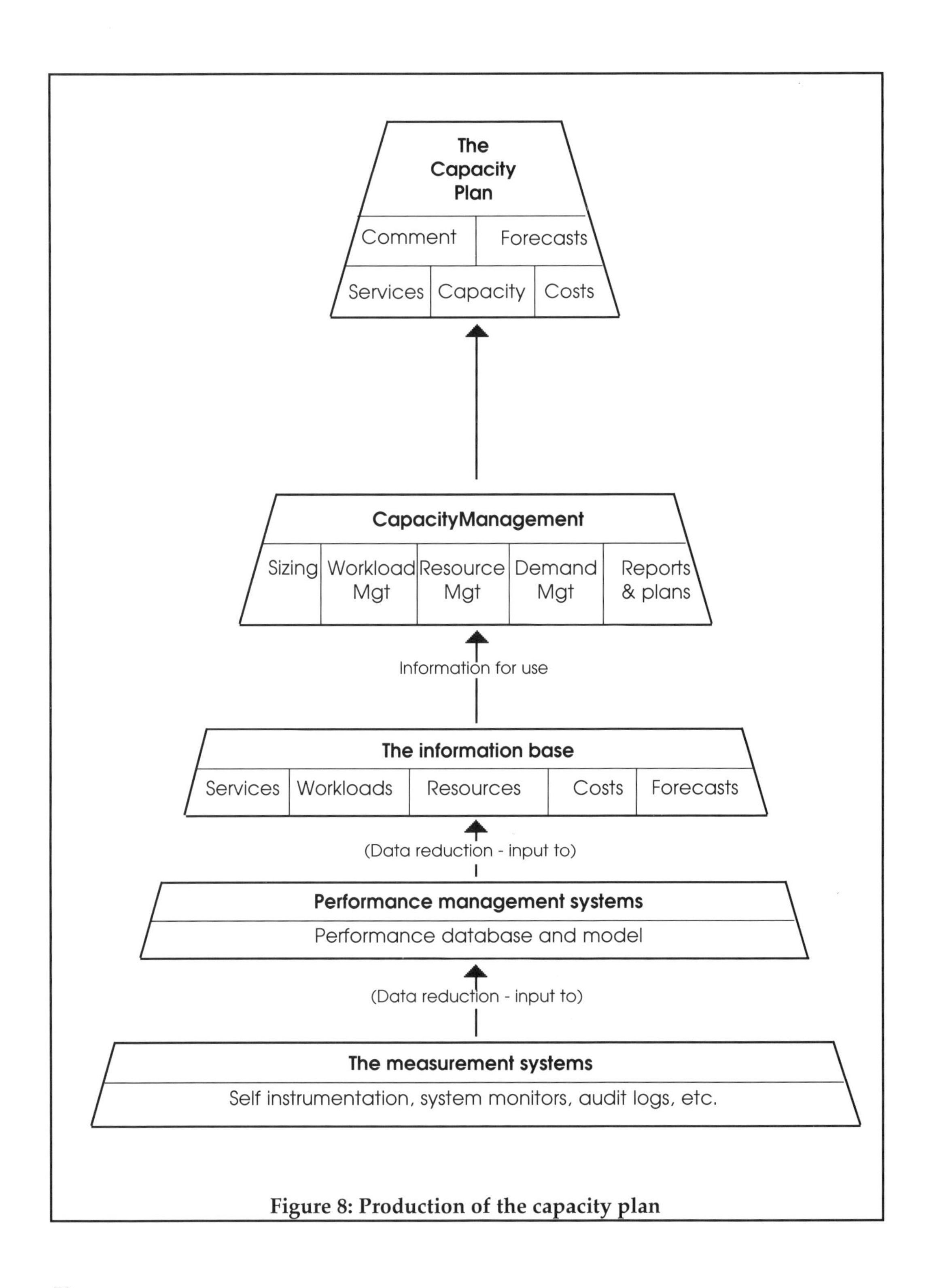

Figure 8: Production of the capacity plan

The Capacity Manager should try to avoid the above situation. The areas of concern typically centre upon the introduction of major new applications or the timings of upgrades. For example senior management may wish to delay an implementation or to phase it in, so that increases in expenditure are controlled; eg the scope of a decision support or office system may be reduced when the full costs are known.

The Capacity Manager should review the current workload forecasts, assess the likely areas of contention and produce a small number of discrete scenarios (3 or 4). Using the current workload forecasts as a base, the Capacity Manager should estimate the hardware and associated costs required at each major milestone over the next twelve months, eg when a new application is implemented, to meet the agreed service levels for each scenario. Use a modelling tool to aid this work.

Present the preliminary findings of this exercise, detailing each scenario with a summary of the implications on service levels and costs, to senior management for discussion. The outcome of this exercise should be an agreed scenario for the plan.

Detailed work

The current set of workload forecasts are used as the basis for detailed work. A minimum of two years' workload forecasts should be modelled. It is usually sufficient to model each quarter separately but it may be necessary in some cases, to do it on a monthly basis.

Feed hypothetical changes in workload demand into the modelling tool until such time as service levels can no longer be met. Then make appropriate changes to the hardware model until the modelling tool indicates that service levels can be achieved.

Note that modelling tools do not calculate disk space requirements. Therefore, the Capacity Manager has to calculate this item manually (or with the aid of a spreadsheet) if it differs from the current set of forecasts. Include any additional disks, controllers and channels which are required to meet the demand for access at the appropriate times in the plan.

As many models are likely to be developed during this exercise, a modelling tool which allows the electronic data input of all the details pertaining to a complete (or partial) plan, and the execution of that plan in its entirety (without user intervention) is beneficial.

Discuss the cost implications of any hardware changes with the Cost Manager.

The capacity plan

It is not possible to provide an in-depth description of a capacity plan; the variation in content that is possible is very large. Instead, this section deals with the key issues. The Capacity Management Primer, published by CCMS Associates, is one useful reference work for those wishing to read more detailed guidance. The production of a plan is summarized in figure 8, page 52.

The capacity plan should be produced initially in draft form for discussion with senior IT management. Identify the owner of the plan: if the plan is not owned by the IT Services Manager or some other senior figure, there is a danger that the plan will not be treated seriously. If the Capacity Manager is a senior figure (which is the case in some organizations) the problem does not arise.

Draw up a distribution list for the plan to include all senior staff. The distribution list should also state the frequency of published updates to the plan (some updates may be used solely by the Capacity Manager to monitor actual versus predicted values).

Plan content

The contents can be grouped under six main headings:

* introduction and commentary
* forecast scenarios
* service summaries
* capacity summaries
* cost summaries
* contingency plan.

Introduction & commentary

The first part of the capacity plan (introduction and commentary) should be a simple global review of how the organization has fared. The global review should summarize important events (eg installation of new hardware) and comment on actual achievements. The level of detail can be increased in the later sections to supplement information provided in the introduction and commentary. In this section include:

* date and version number
* sign-off procedure
* introduction (what the plan contains)

* changes since the last plan
* forecast scenarios
    - business growth
    - function changes
    - hardware, software needs
* service summaries
    - quantity
    - quality
* capacity summaries
    - workload
    - resource
* cost summaries
    - unit costs
    - cost recovery
* contingency plan.

Forecasts

The forecast scenarios are based on information gathered about workload growth in terms of business volumes and new functions. The major subjects should be:

* service descriptions (eg payroll, application development)
* business unit definitions (eg cheques)
* information services
* assumptions
* volumes
* new functions
* new hardware/software needs.

Service summary

Based on the workload forecast scenarios, provide details about the business in terms of:

* classification (eg on line, batch)
* business unit forecasts
* service level targets.

Capacity summary

Document the expected workload growth and its impact on resources based on the forecasts available. This section should be subdivided into predictions of:

* CPU use
* disk use
* disk space use
* tape use
* terminals needed
* network changes
* main memory use
* print use.

Cost summary

This section should describe the expected costs of running the IT services and how predictions about costs matched actual costs. If possible, include information about unit costs (business items) and resource costs (CPU, disks). Produce the cost summary in collaboration with the Cost Manager.

Contingency plan

Produce a separate capacity plan for contingency planning purposes. This is typically a subset of the full plan, in terms of the workloads which are to be supported, and the hardware which is required to provide the necessary levels of service after a disaster.

Produce this plan at the same time as the full plan. It forms an input to contingency planning.

This work is relatively straightforward since it is a logical extension to the production of the full plan.

Format

Consider how best to present numerical information - graphs are usually the best method of presentation. An illustration enables the reader to perceive at a glance whether a critical situation exists. A picture is worth a thousand words only if it is clear and informative. Ensure that graphs are annotated with all relevant information. The layout of the pages should also be considered. Two-page layouts (an illustration on one page and a commentary on the opposite page) can be especially useful. See Annex L for some example illustrations.

Align the publication cycle with the start of the financial year. Review the plan quarterly so that adjustments can be made to budgets forecasts. Finally, ensure that the plan looks professional: use desktop graphics and other publishing tools to produce a quality document.

4.1.7 Service level management

The primary objectives of an interface between CM and SLM are to:

* provide the Service Level Manager with information on estimated service levels which can be achieved for all existing and planned new workloads to assist in the negotiation of service level agreements
* develop a system which monitors and reports actual against agreed service levels and feeds this information into service level management; and when thresholds are breached, to problem management.

The provision of estimated service levels to the Service Level Manager are deliverables from the workload management, application sizing, resource management and modelling activities of capacity management which are all discussed in the appropriate sections elsewhere in section 4.

Several issues should be considered before the implementation of service level monitoring is attempted:

* definition of response times
* monitoring the elements of response time
* definition of batch turnaround times
* monitoring the elements of batch turnaround time.

The service level monitoring reports which are produced should include a daily exception report, a detailed weekly report and a rolling period report eg last 13 weeks. Examples of such reports are shown in Figures 9 and 10.

4.1.8 Cost management

The Capacity Manager must liaise with the Cost Manager about the impact (in terms of cost, or charging policy) of any proposed changes to the hardware and software platform. In particular, liaison can occur about workload management, application sizing, resource management and the production of the capacity plan. These interfaces are dealt with under the appropriate headings elsewhere in section 4.

SERVICE LEVEL MONITORING DAILY EXCEPTION REPORT FOR 3/2/90

ONLINE/REGULAR BATCH

USER	SYSTEM	SLA NO	TIME FROM	TIME TO	FREQ. OF USE	% OF FREQ. SL EXCEEDED
Accounts	GL	AC012	1100	1200	5200	21
Accounts	GL	ACC12	1500	1600	4920	20
Personnel	PE	PE007	1500	1600	3719	29
Development	Batch	DV002	1100	1200	65	32

SERVICE LEVEL MONITORING DAILY EXCEPTION REPORT FOR 3/2/90

BATCH

USER	SYSTEM	SLA NO	JOBNAME	COMMENTS
Accounts	GL	AC012	Trial Balance	Tape Fail

SERVICE LEVEL MONITORING DAILY EXCEPTION REPORT FOR 3/2/90

NON-AVAILABILITY INCIDENTS

USER	SYSTEM	SLA NO	TIMES UNAVAILABLE FROM	TO	COMMENTS
Accounts	GL	AC012	0930	1015	Cluster Controller
	PL	AC013	0930	1015	Cluster Controller

Figure 9: Daily exception reports

SERVICE LEVEL MONITORING SUMMARY FOR 3/2/90-9/2/90

ONLINE/REGULAR BATCH

USER	SYSTEM	SLA NO	SUB IDENT. UPDATES	FREQ. OF USE	% SL ACHIEVED
Accounts	GL	AC012	Enquiries	192,712	92
			Updates	59,871	87
Accounts	PL	AC013		61,010	96
Development	Batch	DV002		5,217	82

SERVICE LEVEL MONITORING SUMMARY FOR 3/2/90-9/2/90

AVAILABILITY

USER	SYSTEM	SLA NO	% AVAILABILITY
Accounts	GL	ACC12	96.2
Personnel	PE	PE007	98.6

Figure 10: Weekly exception reports

Another aspect of this interface for capacity management is to store sufficient accounting data so that cost management can account for all costs and, in an equitable manner allocate costs (and, optionally, charge for the use of resources).

The Capacity Manager should ensure that all users of resources can be uniquely identified. This is achieved by confirming that adequate naming conventions are employed. Note that difficulties may be encountered, particularly on batch jobs where the output may go to several distinct users.

The Capacity Manager should ensure that adequate data items are collected on resource usage for each transaction or job. Items will include some or all of the following for each cost centre:

* CPU time used
* number of I/Os performed
* amount of memory used
* elapsed time for job
* connect time for online session
* number of terminal I/Os
* number of print lines
* number of tape mounts
* amount of disk space used
* number of tapes which are kept
* number of transactions
* number of jobs
* time of day or shift
* job class
* any other items which may be required by cost management.

The Capacity Manager should ensure that sufficient historical data is maintained, not only for current costing and charging purposes, but also to assist the Cost Manager to predict future costs and charges.

4.1.9 The order of implementation

Sections 4.1.1 through to 4.1.6 address each of the major activities of capacity management in some detail, without discussing the chronological order in which the main tasks can logically be tackled.

There is no single solution to this problem. The approach depends upon the size of the installation, its complexity (single or multiple systems), and the degree of change to which it is subjected at the time of implementation (the scope of new development).

However, a typical order is:

* performance monitoring
* identification of workloads
* identification of working patterns and peaks
* the setting up of the CDB to collect technical and business data
* production of management reports on the current period and on historical trends
* forecasting
* definition of service levels
* production of the capacity plan.

Figure 11 shows a hypothetical project plan for the first year of capacity management. It could apply to a medium-sized organization in capacity terms; eg IBM low-end 3090, ICL 3965/80 or DEC high-end 6500/9000, where one person is responsible for performance management with a full-time person responsible for capacity planning.

Performance monitoring should commence immediately. Some work will probably already have been done in this area, even if it has only been done on an *ad hoc* basis. Monitoring of the key hardware components on an hourly basis will suffice in the short-term.

This is followed by the development of a daily reporting system (see Annex C) which leaves more time for the performance analyst to concentrate on tuning and other relevant matters.

The identification of workloads should precede the creation of the CDB since it has a bearing on the content of the database.

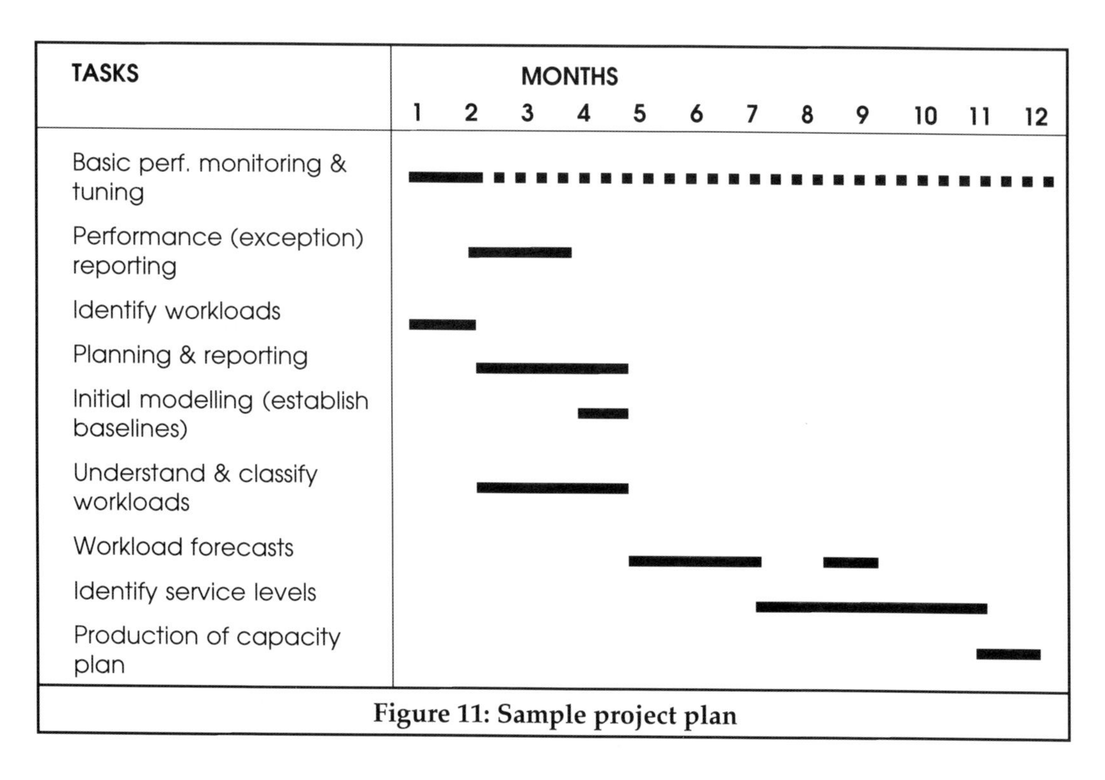

Figure 11: Sample project plan

The CDB may be just a collection of discrete files, rather than a sophisticated, integrated database unless a DBMS (Database Management System) has been purchased, perhaps for application development. The Capacity Manager should concentrate initially on the development of a functional but effective system. For example, technical items might be kept in the form which they were originally output by the monitor(s). The Performance Manager creates the CDB (as he/she will be responsible for its integrity and maintenance) after discussion with the Capacity Manager.

Meanwhile, the Capacity Manager, having identified the workloads, is now observing the system to discover what the working patterns are and when the peaks occur. The first draft of the workload catalogue is assembled and the resource profiles of the major transactions/jobs are derived.

The next step is to perform the first forecasting exercise. Expect this to take longer than subsequent iterations of forecasts.

When there are forecasts, based on existing workloads and sizing of new workloads, service level management can be addressed. Refer to the ITIL module **Service Level Management**.

Meanwhile, the second set of forecasts are produced. This set is then used as the foundation for the production of the first capacity plan.

No mention has been made in this hypothetical scenario of cost management or resource management. Cost management is indirectly dealt with: the requirement for information on the use of hardware resources is addressed during the creation of the CDB. Also, the Capacity Manager will liaise with the Cost Manager during the forecasting and capacity planning phases.

It is important that the project plan for the introduction of capacity management is not too ambitious as there will undoubtedly be a requirement to perform some *ad hoc* studies during this period, although they should be kept to a minimum.

In this hypothetical scenario, year two will include the full implementation of service levels, the introduction of application sizing and the general refinement of the overall system. Do not forget alignment of the introduction of the capacity management processes to an appropriate time in the financial year.

4.1.10 *Ad hoc* studies

The main emphasis so far in this section has been on the implementation of regular tasks. However, there will also be requests from senior management to perform *ad hoc* studies. These tasks may include investigations on:

* how long can a CPU upgrade be put off?
* the comparison of benefits/costs of various upgrade options to the host I/O subsystem
* the best network upgrade path to improve performance for a specific user
* determination of the effects on cost and performance of major network changes, such as how best to implement a nationwide Job Centre system.

The deliverables from such studies take the form of short reports containing results of analysis of current performance data and model results, and will be technical in nature.

Although *ad hoc* studies need technical background information, the results must be business oriented, otherwise they will not be understood by senior management; technical jargon must be avoided.

Thus they must deal in terms of:

* timescales to implement
* business advantage gained
* investment required
* costs
* equipment lifetime

and must provide options for senior management decisions.

4.2 Dependencies

Commitment to a service oriented approach is arguably the overriding requirement for successful implementation. It is needed from all parties, particularly customers, senior management and IT management. Lack of service oriented approach typically leads to lack of planning information with the resultant adverse impact on the deliverables of capacity management.

There will always be pressure on capacity management to produce early deliverables. This factor should be taken into account during the initial study. Resist any pressure to cut timescales. If the implementation falls behind schedule, then it may be necessary to rework the implementation plan, possibly producing a capacity plan by forecasting at a higher level in the short-term, in order to maintain confidence.

4.2.1 Host (mainframe) organization

Lack of resources within the capacity management team will endanger the implementation dates. Consider the use of external staff, contractors or consultants, to solve this problem. Otherwise, review and revise the project plan.

Information needs

Capacity management requires satisfactory measurements of the current service levels and utilization of all hardware resources; ie adequate monitoring and reporting systems. It also requires adequate and timely information (workload forecasts, hardware demand, and so on) on which to base forecasts and capacity plans.

Tools

Adequate performance monitoring tools are required.

Where service levels are employed, the use of a modelling tool is a prerequisite for the prediction of response times/ batch turnaround times.

Access to commonly used office automation facilities is required to produce professional reports; eg word processing, spreadsheets and graphics.

4.2.2 Network

This sub-section draws together the requirements mentioned in section 3 for effective and beneficial network capacity management.

Organization

Service level management relies on effective network capacity planning working in conjunction with host capacity planning to determine the resources required to satisfy user requirements.

Effective liaison between staff responsible for data and voice networking is required to avoid conflicts of interest and inefficient circuit management.

Information

Network capacity management needs regular measurement of line and network equipment utilizations, information on applications message sizes, transaction volumes, equipment performance characteristics, equipment locations, network topologies and costs.

Tools

Terminal access to the network database is required for extraction of data and analysis of network performance statistics.

Computer based tools, in particular those used for regular and frequent modelling of network performance and costs are essential. Word processing and spreadsheet facilities are also required to produce reports.

4.3 People

The relationships between staff involved directly or indirectly with capacity management have been fully discussed throughout this guidance.

4.4 Timing

Order of implementation is covered in 4.1.9: to summarize, monitoring of existing capacity and performance is required for the maintenance of service levels. Therefore set it up as soon as possible and run on a continuous basis, producing the monthly status reports already described.

Produce the initial capacity plan during the first year and base the implementation plan around that requirement.

5. Post-implementation and audit

5.1 Procedures

The post-implementation processes involve keeping the capacity management systems under review, to ensure that they are working as specified; and ensuring that the systems are regularly audited for efficiency and effectiveness and for compliance to the chosen procedures. So far as the performance management processes are concerned, emphasize the prevention of performance crises; this is achieved by judicious use of exception reporting.

5.1.1 Performance

Although the emphasis is on prevention, there will be occasional performance crises. The use of a real-time monitor (see 7.1) is beneficial to identify the offending items and resolve the immediate problem. Successful performance management can be measured by the reduced incidence of crises, ie a reduction will be expected following introduction of performance management.

Any tuning work which is carried out must be thoroughly tested before it is implemented and should be controlled by change management.

5.1.2 CDB

Review the information held in the CDB to ensure that it is of use. In addition, identify (from workload trends etc) whether or not additional information is needed to enhance the content of the CDB. The CDB must be the central repository for capacity management information. The CDB is a success if the Capacity Manager does not have to look elsewhere for capacity management information to complete forecasts and plans.

5.1.3 Reporting

The main emphasis of management reporting should be on the production of a limited set of reports covering the current period, historical trends and forecasts. Wherever possible, they should relate to the business and to the level of service which is being provided to customers. Use graphs in preference to tabulations since most managers prefer to use a graph.

When reports can be produced which show both planned and actual data, capacity management reports are a success.

Although prototype reports are produced during the initial study, it is probable that the suitability of the reports will not become fully apparent for 3-6 months after implementation. Capacity management should seek feedback from the recipients of the reports after 3 months and change the reports, as appropriate.

Isolate requests for more detailed information on specific applications and deal with them separately by maintaining a list of outstanding reports to be tackled as time permits.

The number and variety of reports will inevitably increase, despite attempts to keep them to manageable levels. In this situation, capacity management should consider moving away from paper-based reports. Reports can be stored on the host or on a PC where they can be viewed by the recipients.

5.1.4 Workload forecasting

Perform workload forecasting quarterly, looking forward through a two-year window on a quarter by quarter basis.

Discussion with the users, IT management and other relevant parties, is the foundation for forecasting. Incorporate meetings with the users into the SLA reviews, where possible.

Deliver the results of each forecasting exercise as a written report (as detailed in section 4). Apart from future predictions the report should show how successful or otherwise previous forecasts have been by comparing them against actuals. It is important to explain the reason for any identified variance from forecasts. The successful Capacity Manager will produce reports which show little variance between forecast values and actuals. The Capacity Manager should seek feedback from the recipients of this report with regard to its suitability and make alterations where appropriate.

There will be a learning curve for all concerned. It can be difficult for users to predict future requirements, especially when they have had no previous exposure to this activity. As stated in section 4, the Capacity Manager should be prepared to lead the user by suggesting possible minima and maxima. Historical trend reports on volumes can assist the process. Eventually, both customers' and the Capacity Manager's confidence will grow as actual resource usage can be compared with the initial sets of forecasts, thus providing information on the relative strengths of the original estimates. It is likely to take a year before the full benefits of the forecasting process are fully realized.

Ensure that the capacity management team understands the relevance of any new workloads and new applications which might be needed to process the new workloads.

Application sizing

Although the application development standards may have to be reviewed and possibly amended to provide capacity management with the information required, do not assume that the information will be produced, particularly in the early days. To overcome this possible problem the Capacity Manager should ensure that application developers are aware of all development activity from the time of project inception. Close liaison with the Application Development Manager and the Change Manager may assist this process. SSADM V4 helps to ensure that applications developers provide the relevant information to capacity management in the early stages of project development.

When a new application development has been identified, the Capacity Manager should discuss capacity management's requirements for information with the Project Manager, identifying and addressing any difficulties, eg lack of volumetric data. The Capacity Manager should be prepared to give a 'Capacity Management Awareness' presentation (3.1.6.11) to the members of the project team so that they understand the need for application sizing and its role within capacity management. Such presentations are necessary until all development staff comprehend the need and role of application sizing.

Discuss the results of all sizing exercises with the project team so that they obtain feedback on the performance implications of the proposed system.

Post-implementation reviews of new applications should include an assessment of the sizing work which was carried out, include the accuracy of the volumetric data which was provided to capacity management and the accuracy of the sizing results. Use all findings to refine and improve the application sizing methodology.

5.1.5 The capacity plan

Produce a capacity plan annually prior to the preparation of budgets for the coming financial year. Relate the forecasts of usage, predicted levels of service and associated costs to the businesses. A more detailed breakdown of the plan, eg by individual workload or application, should also be provided.

Update the capacity plan quarterly. The main purpose of this is to act as a checkpoint, highlighting any unexpected changes and their implications. The results can then be used in any budgetary revisions.

5.1.6 Service level management

Review the suitability of the service level monitoring reporting system (eg daily exception reports and weekly summaries) with the Service Level Manager and alter where necessary.

Review the accuracy and timeliness of capacity management input to the negotiation of SLAs.

It is vitally important that the Service Level Manager is apprised of all relevant information regarding customer requests for specific levels of service. Too often a customer request for a specific level of service is accepted without question. The service levels are linked to cost; the cost ultimately is reflected in charges to customers. Where service levels are requested which cannot be attained (even at a cost which can be calculated) it is the job of the Capacity Manager to explain why the service levels are unattainable.

5.1.7 Cost management

The Capacity Manager must continually liaise with the Cost Manager to discuss the cost implications of any upgrades which are considered necessary as a result of any forecasting, sizing or capacity planning exercise. As was mentioned in 5.1.6, some service level requests may need to be costed.

In addition, the Capacity Manager should liaise with the Cost Manager to review the availability of sufficient accounting data on resource usage, to facilitate the allocation of costs and to meet any requirement for charging.

5.1.8 Demand management

Given commitment from senior management (Business and IT), the Capacity Manager can be one of the most influential managers in the organization. The Capacity Manager is aware of workloads, costs, available capacity, required service levels and the exigencies of the business. A credible capacity management team, one which has provided reasonably accurate sizing models, one which can quickly and reasonably accurately assess the impact of new or changed workloads, should be made responsible for the task of demand management.

Demand management is the management of customer demand for IT, in the face of IT cutbacks, insufficient hardware, perhaps even a processing disaster or unforeseen workload growth. There may even be periodic peaks for which the Capacity Manager has deliberately not catered.

Business priorities in the event of crises should have been decided by a senior user/IT committee. The Capacity Manager should be aware of the priorities and have delegated responsibility to manage resources to meet the business priorities. If the Capacity Manager is not given this responsibility by the IT Directorate, it is likely that all customers could be affected by a crisis. The Capacity Manager needs to be knowledgeable enough to respond to a crisis and most importantly, be aware that any decisions made will be backed by IT management.

Performance crises are discussed further in Appendix C: the Capacity Manager may be able to recommend reducing demand by, for example, limiting the number of concurrent on-line users or batch streams. Few options which are available to reduce demand could be considered to be popular. It is for that reason that the Capacity Manager must have commitment from senior management: the entire organization must also be aware of that commitment.

Long-term demand management (perhaps required because the need for a new mainframe was not recognized quickly enough) can seriously affect the credibility of the IT Directorate. Customers - and the business - suffer and it is usual that the image of IT in the organization is tarnished. Long-term demand management requires the IT Directorate to take unpopular measures: one method of limiting the damage to the image of IT is to keep customers fully informed about the performance crises, the reasons and the anticipated solutions. And, of course, the timescale for the solutions. Once more, the Capacity Manager should be at the forefront of any publicity campaign regarding such crises.

The Capacity Manager is not a technician. The Capacity Manager should be technically aware and have access to first rate technicians but above all else, the Capacity Manager must be a communicator, a person who can understand the needs of the business and the demands of the business on IT. When the Capacity Manager is faced with a crisis which affects the needs of the business, it is necessary to manage the demand, by artificially constraining it and accepting degraded levels of service. Occasionally, it might become necessary to suspend or renegotiate a SLA (accepting any penalty clauses which may be invoked by customers) because the number of transactions or jobs is too large to be supported on the infrastructure. SLAs define the usual demands of users. SLAs should also outline the policy for curtailing excessive demand.

Where possible, persuade some customers to use the system outside known peak periods when performance is better. If a chargeback system is in operation, the use of the system during off-peak periods can be made more attractive by reduced rates.

5.1.9 Auditing for effectiveness

It is complacent to implement any system and expect the objectives, methods and deliverables to remain inviolate for the foreseeable future. Review the effectiveness of capacity management on a regular basis.

The main questions which should be posed are:

* do management accept and implement capacity management recommendations? (If not, then investigate the effectiveness of communication, both oral and written. In addition, check management's understanding of capacity management and its role in the overall IS strategy. Without commitment to capacity management at a high level, many of the benefits of implementing capacity management will not be realized)

* is there adequate capacity to enable provision of the agreed level of service to customers? (If the answer is no, examine the understanding of current resource usage, the methods of forecasting, sizing and the modelling techniques)

* is the right information provided, in the right format, at the right time, to the right people? (Elicit feedback from everyone concerned, subsequently investigate any adverse comment and rectify the situation, where possible).

Section 5.1.10 covers auditing for compliance and many of the bullet points apply equally to auditing capacity management for effectiveness.

5.1.10 Auditing for compliance

This sub-section will enable organizations to audit their capacity management function, using an independent auditor, for compliance to the procedures and advice in this module. It is recommended that such an audit be completed annually, or more frequently where local circumstances and problems dictate. Checks should be carried out to ensure that:

* communication with all relevant people takes place and is effective
* sufficient monitors are in place to allow all major aspects of the system to be observed in an effective manner
* detailed monitoring studies are performed regularly (at least once a fortnight) or more frequently in prolonged periods of poor performance
* performance problems are rectified or minimized within agreed timescales
* the potential benefits of any major tuning exercise are quantified prior to commencement of the work, and the actual benefits are also recorded afterwards
* the content of the CDB is appropriate for capacity management purposes
* regular checks are carried out to ensure the integrity of the CDB, eg there are no instances of missing data or duplicated data
* all agreed reports are produced according to the agreed schedules
* a workload catalogue is in existence and there are procedures for updating it
* workload forecasting is carried out quarterly and looks forward up to the planning horizon (minimum of two years)
* forecasting is based on the customer's estimates for future usage, historical trends, current resource usage, and information from IT management
* forecasts are published and discussed with customers

* application sizing is an integral part of the application development lifecycle and is carried out at all appropriate stages of the lifecycle (if SSADM is in use, ensure that the appropriate SSADM/ Capacity Planning guide is in use)
* the results from all application sizing exercises (hardware utilizations, levels of service and cost implications) are distributed to IT management, the project team, the Service Level Manager and the Cost Manager
* the Service Level Manager is provided with sufficient information on volumes, resource usage and likely service levels to allow him/her to negotiate SLAs
* the service level reporting system provides an effective mechanism for monitoring service levels
* timely information regarding upgrades and redundant equipment is relayed to the Cost Manager
* the requirements of cost management are catered for, in terms of completeness of accounting data for resource usage
* the Capacity Manager keeps up-to-date with changes in technology and assesses the possible benefits
* a capacity plan is produced annually to a specific agreed deadline, to provide input to the business planning cycle
* where required, a separate disaster capacity plan is produced as a by-product from the full capacity plan
* interfaces to other supporting processes, (availability management, contingency planning, help desk, problem and change management) exist and are effective
* all procedures and operating instructions are documented.

5.2 Dependencies

IT management must convince the IT Director and the management board that capacity management provides benefit, and therefore has an important role in the IT business.

Commitment is also required from users, IT management and IT personnel. People are naturally impatient to see deliverables. Recognize that it will take some time for capacity management, users and other parties, to gain the experience which is necessary for the maximum benefits to be realized. This is most noticeable in the area of forecasting. The more forecasting exercises that are carried out, the better users become at supplying the base input figures, and the more accurate are the results produced by the capacity planners. Therefore, the Capacity Manager should attempt to get individuals to retain their enthusiasm. He/she should not fail to produce deliverables of satisfactory quality by the promised dates.

Capacity management must have systematic procedures to obtain all necessary information, viz:

* details of current performance
* service level requirements
* details of new applications
* customer's future requirements
* IT direction (eg move towards office automation)
* information on new technology.

5.3 People

The Help Desk is responsible for recording and forwarding to the Capacity Manager, details of any incidents which relate to unsatisfactory performance.

The Availability Manager will liaise with the Capacity Manager with reference to all instances of non-availability which are due to performance problems.

The Network and Host Capacity Managers must liaise in order to provide a seamless service.

The Network Capacity Manager must have regular meetings with the Voice Network Manager to harmonize circuit management methods and provision.

The Change Manager must liaise with the Capacity Manager to ensure that any proposed changes do not adversely affect existing service levels. Note that changes which are requested by the Capacity Manager must be subject to change management.

The Capacity Manager must liaise with external bodies, with respect to hardware and software performance issues, to gain knowledge of the performance implications of products. External bodies includes hardware and software vendors, user groups and other organizations which use similar hardware and software products.

5.4 Timing

Timing considerations have been discussed as appropriate in the sub-section Auditing for compliance (5.1.10).

6. Benefits, costs and possible problems

6.1 Benefits

The introduction of capacity management is beneficial to an organization. This is demonstrable, but it is up to the Capacity Manager to prove that the cost of introducing capacity management is outweighed by the benefits to be accrued. There are usually improvements in efficiency, effectiveness and economy, all of which can be quantified and demonstrated.

6.1.1 Reduced risk and increased efficiency

The major benefits of capacity management are reduction of risks and increased efficiency: good capacity management will ensure that sufficient IT capacity is available at all times to run the organization's required workload, including application development work, as the workloads evolve. That in turn reduces the risk that the IT Directorate may be unable, through lack of capacity, to provide the quality IT services that are needed to support organizations' businesses.

6.1.2 Cost savings

A particular benefit of capacity management is that it leads to cost savings, including:

* the ability to expand capabilities within budgets
* the IT Directorate's provision of better services, which help organizations' businesses to operate more efficiently and effectively (eg on-line response to customer enquiries)
* IT capacity costs are contained or reduced, because there is no excess capacity and capacity is used efficiently (ie all expenditure justified by plans and forecasts)
* low-cost performance improvements can sometimes be identified which contribute to economical provision of services
* planned buying is cheaper than panic buying!

6.1.3 Other benefits

Customer relations

Capacity management helps IT Directorates to provide services that have good and consistent performance. Good and consistent performance ensures good relationships with IT customers, whether they be direct users or businesses that are dependent on the IT Directorate. Poor service also affects an organization's relationship with its customers: capacity management helps to reduce this risk.

Appropriate service levels

Capacity management helps IT Directorates to specify the appropriate levels of service performance and throughput - levels that represent a cost-effective balance between adequate service quality and a service which can cope with all potential peak workloads.

Using capacity management, the cost of providing better performance (for example, improved terminal response times) can be assessed against the likely benefits to an organization's business.

Timing of upgrades

Capacity management helps the IT Directorate to optimize the timing and building of hardware upgrades: capacity is increased when it is required and by the right amount, rather than by too much too soon or by too little too late.

Confident forecasts

Capacity management helps the IT Directorate to forecast accurately the performance and throughput of existing and new services as user demands change.

Efficient use of personnel

When the frustration caused by performance and capacity problems is reduced, more efficient use can be made of IT staff time. Their time is better spent on planning than on 'fire-fighting'.

Anticipation of problems

Potential performance and capacity problems can be anticipated, and corrective action instigated to prevent a crisis.

Better understanding and awareness

Capacity management helps the IT Directorate to understand their IT infrastructures and increases the awareness of the IT Directorate about the importance of SLAs.

All of the benefits described above should be available to the organization. To demonstrate the benefits, institute metrics to measure improvements. For example, identify when hardware upgrades were deferred (or expedited) because of capacity management. Measure the savings accrued because of the intervention.

6.2 Costs

The costs associated with a capacity management function must be estimated at the planning stage as detailed in section 3.1.6.10. Briefly, these costs can be categorized under two main headings, staff and products.

Staff

The basic staff costs depend on the number of staff that are needed to support the size of organization and IT infrastructure in question. As an example, two people are probably needed on a site which has an ICL 3980, IBM 3090, or cluster of VAXs with 3-4 processor nodes.

Expect to use staff graded at lower to middle management level - in government terms SEO or HEO grades, although in larger organizations where the workload is subject to heavy development or where the business is critically dependent on IT, higher graded staff may be needed. The British Computer Society industry model for capacity management (included in the Professional Development Scheme material) is useful reference material for grading advice. Include training and conference costs although they are likely to be relatively low.

Products

Include all costs for additional software products. For example monitors and data manipulation, reporting (spreadsheets, word processors, graph-drawing packages) and modelling tools. Add the cost of any additional hardware which may be required to run those software products, particularly PCs and special output hardware.

Tools

Expect each member of the team to have their own PC with associated software and, potentially shared, printing facilities.

6.3 Possible problems

This section describes a number of possible problems associated with capacity management, as it applies to hosts (6.3.1) and networks (6.3.2).

6.3.1 Hosts

Over-expectation

Beware of over-expectation of the benefits which may be gained from tuning: computers are finite resources and as the old adage will have it, "you cannot fit a quart into a pint pot". The savings which can be made through tuning are not normally great. Sometimes a one-off saving is possible. If a large saving is identified through a tuning exercise investigate closely other areas within IT such as the application or database design processes. Usually, the tuning has simply disguised or ameliorated poor design.

The rescheduling of workloads, in order that peaks may be smoothed out and upgrades thus delayed, may not be easy, particularly when online systems are crucial during the normal working day.

Customer expectation

Customer expectation usually exceeds technical reality. The Capacity Manager must educate all customers on the technical feasibility and cost implications of meeting any over-ambitious requirements. For new applications, make the customer aware of likely response times, throughputs and turnaround times at the earliest possible time within the development cycle. Also, make application developers aware, early in the development cycle, of the impact of their proposed design on the level of service that can be provided to users of the new application and existing applications. (5.1.4)

Vendor influence

Vendors tend to quote throughput estimates which are based on benchmarks which, often, cannot be achieved by commercial applications. In particular, use the transactions per second (TPS) rates which many vendors quote from running the Debit/Credit card benchmark only as a coarse guide to comparing the products of several vendors.

Ideally, sizing should be the responsibility of an organization's Capacity Manager: do not devolve this work to vendors without good reason.

Lack of information

It is difficult to obtain the initial information needed, particularly on future customer workloads, to do capacity planning. However, reasonable results can be produced from quite crude estimates. In subsequent iterations of the planning cycle, aim to improve the accuracy of the data, which has corresponding beneficial effects on the accuracy of the capacity plan. The Capacity Manager must stress that service levels cannot be maintained in a cost-effective manner if the required information is not available at the right level of detail.

The problems described for host computers also apply to networks.

6.3.2 Networks

It is difficult at present to gather sufficient performance statistics on local area networks, since few of the current generation of PC-based file servers, bridges and gateways produce adequate data. This will improve as the technology changes. In the meantime, carry out performance benchmarks on these devices and perform trend analysis using a model based on the benchmark data.

There may be demarcation disputes between voice and data network management as to where responsibility lies for planning and procurement of network equipment. A classic case of difficulty is links between hosts and the TELEX network, since the latter has traditionally been the domain of voice telecommunications. This problem can only be resolved by setting up a single management point. If voice telecommunications is managed by the IT Directorate, coordination can be achieved by line management instruction. Otherwise, a joint steering group needs to be set up to take overall responsibility for the network.

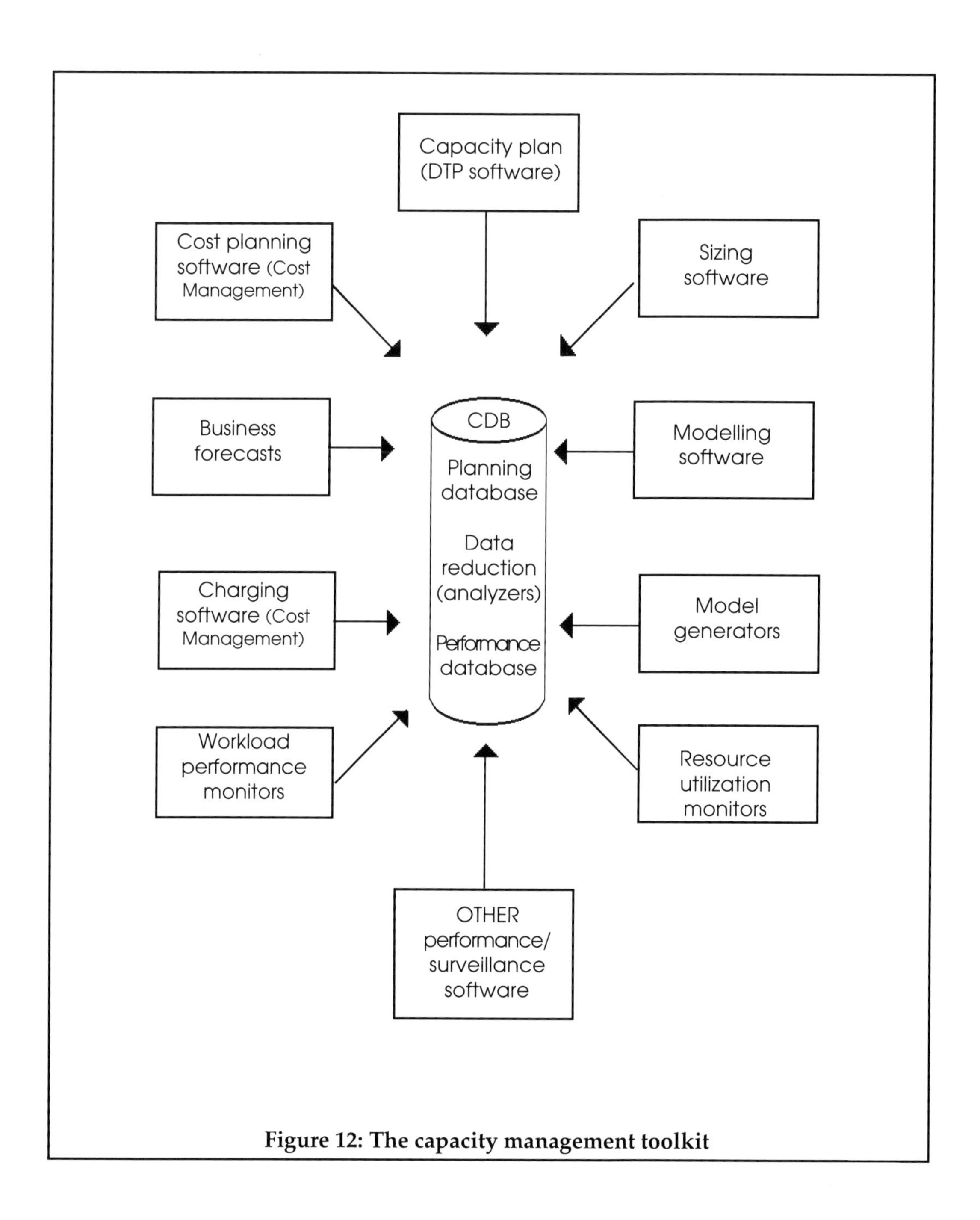

Figure 12: The capacity management toolkit

7. Tools

This section deals with the support tools which may be required for capacity management. Examples are given of some of the products which are currently available in the marketplace. New and improved products are continually appearing and therefore it is incumbent on the organization to supplement its understanding of the marketplace, prior to the commencement of any evaluation of the tools.

Figure 12, opposite, illustrates the requirements of a capacity management toolkit.

7.1 Host monitoring

Host monitoring can be achieved using standard time-driven monitors which provide details of how the hardware is being utilized. They function by sampling various aspects of the environment (eg CPU, input/output(I/O) devices and controllers) at predefined intervals, and periodically writing the information to tape or disk. This data can be interrogated to produce reports, generally in batch mode although some monitors have a real-time display capability. System-wide items which can be monitored and reported typically include:

* CPU utilization
* I/O rates and utilization of each device
* controller (and channel) utilizations
* paging (VSI) rates and optionally physical I/Os
* swapping (RIRO) rates and optionally physical I/Os
* use of real memory.

In addition, the monitors typically provide information on CPU, I/O and paging rates at a more detailed level. The precise level varies, according to the operating system. For example, IBM MVS systems provide such detail at performance group level, ICL VME at policy level, and Digital's VMS at the process level.

These standard monitors, provided by hardware suppliers, can be supplemented by third-party products. They typically provide additional functionality:

* superior real-time capability
* more items monitored

* better reporting capability; eg exception reporting
* reports give greater level of detail.

Examples of third-party products include Candle's products (IBM), Landmark's products (IBM), Phoenix's PDR (ICL), Ultracomp's SCEPTRE (ICL), CIS's QUANTUM PM (DEC VAX), Software Intelligence's RABBIT 2 (DEC VAX) and ROSEBUD (STRATUS).

Host monitoring can also be achieved using event-driven monitors, which as the name implies, record information when a specified event such as logging on/off or program/job termination occurs. This type of data is typically given the generic title, "Accounting Data" since it can be used to allocate costs or charge users for resources which have been consumed.

Accounting data is provided as a standard offering by the majority of mainframe and minicomputer manufacturers. However, the reporting facilities tend to be basic and third-party vendors tend to concentrate on the manipulation and exploitation of this type of data, eg chargeback systems. Examples of third-party products include Legent's BDBF and MICS ACCOUNTING OPTION (IBM), Pace's KOMMAND III (IBM), Phoenix's GAP (The Government Accounting package under licence from CCTA for ICL VME systems), Software Intelligence's RABBIT 7 (DEC VAX) and CIS's QUANTUM RS (DEC VAX). In addition, most of the third-party host monitors have the capability to access accounting data.

7.2 Data manipulation and reporting

The use of a capacity management database (CDB) has been recommended throughout this module. Therefore, a language which allows data to be stored, retrieved, manipulated, displayed in graphical form and reported in a flexible manner is advantageous. The SAS products (from the SAS Institute) are popular in the area of capacity management. They run on a number of hardware platforms, such as IBM, DEC, Prime and Data General. There is also a PC version which contains most of the functionality of the mainframe and minicomputer versions, although performance may not be as good.

Use may be made of fourth generation language products which the installation may have already purchased for development purposes. Evaluate such products for ease of use, speed of development and the ability to interface to the monitors and products which have been mentioned in section 7.1 above.

Plan production can be achieved using generally available items of software, eg spreadsheets, word processing and desk top publishing packages. Where possible, capacity management should use those software products which are regarded as standard within the organization.

7.3 Network database

The Network Database (CDB) is a critical resource to network capacity management, therefore ensure the database is available from the outset. Since this database is accessed by a number of staff with different aims and needs and it contains many different kinds of information, it should be relational and should have good *ad hoc* querying facilities. For these reasons, a database which uses the SQL (Structured Query Language) interface is recommended.

The database is likely to occupy several megabytes of disk storage. It will also expand over time as performance statistics are gathered. Its final size is difficult to predict; much depends on the availability and detail of the performance statistics gathered, and the degree to which weeding of older statistics is performed. Thus consider the database as a candidate for a mainframe system. The best solution depends upon the existing facilities and needs of the organization concerned.

A good database design is important to ensure good performance, flexible retrieval and update.

7.4 Network monitoring

Real-time links to network performance monitoring facilities are not required for capacity management but may be needed by Network Operations to meet their day-to-day operational responsibilities. Obtain performance statistics from the Network Database to avoid unnecessary duplication of the processes of data extraction and reduction, which may affect system performance. However, Network Operations need tools to provide not only satisfactory network management but also to supply the information to the Network Database required for capacity management.

For mainframes, considerable facilities exist for network monitoring. For IBM there is NetView, while for ICL there is Community Management. These products are supplemented by third-party packages, and may be replaced by them. For example, the Cincom NetMaster product provides a popular NetView alternative.

However, there are significant disadvantages in these offerings in that they are manufacturer-specific. An open systems policy provides the best way forward if hybrid tools are required by the organization. IBM has attempted to address open systems with NetView/PC, an interface to third-party devices. Also, some network equipment manufacturers (eg Timeplex) provide NetView interfaces.

Almost all of the major communications equipment suppliers (CASE, RACAL, Motorola, Timeplex, Infotron, Plessey, to mention just a few) have their own proprietary network management (ie monitoring/remote operation) systems. The most modern of these have ready-built interfaces to computer systems for data consolidation. Even those without ready-built interfaces have a terminal interface which can be used to provide computer data capture if the necessary software is written and the computer link made.

ISO is addressing the area of network management for OSI networks by defining CMIP (common management interface protocol) and CMIS (common management information service). Standards ISO 9596 and ISO 9595 refer respectively to these definitions.

The situation for heterogeneous networks is currently unsatisfactory. Implementation of comprehensive network monitoring is therefore likely to involve writing software for data capture and consolidation on the host computer.

Likely components of a comprehensive monitoring system are:

* a modem management system, for detecting line error rates and failures at the physical level (OSI layer 1)

* a time-division multiplexer management system for monitoring errors and utilizations of links and nodes (OSI layer 2)

* a statistical multiplexer/packet switch management system for monitoring traffic, allowing reconfiguration and traffic re-routing and for detecting errors up to network level (OSI layer 3)
* a host computer management system for monitoring traffic, allowing management of proprietary network equipment up to the application level (OSI layer 7)
* a LAN monitor such as provided by Microsoft LAN Manager or Novell.

The choice of tools in each case is almost entirely dictated by what the individual manufacturer can supply.

7.5 Host modelling

Host modelling tools are concerned with modelling of the central computer configuration. They do not model the network which is discussed in section 7.7.

The main advantage of host modelling tools is their ability to calculate predicted hardware utilizations, queueing times and hence response/ turnaround times, based on user forecasts for each workload such as throughput, terminal population or batch job concurrency.

There are two main methods of modelling: simulation and analytic techniques. Simulation is used to model discrete events within the software and hardware environment. Input to a simulation model can be time-consuming (weeks or even months for very large systems). However, the results can be extremely accurate. Therefore, if very high levels of accuracy are required, a simulation modelling tool is most appropriate. Pinnacle's SCERT II is an example of a simulation modelling tool.

Before using a simulation modelling tool, ensure that the data to hand is very accurate or you will be wasting your time using such a tool.

By contrast, analytic modelling tools are based on standard algorithms, most of which were developed in the late sixties and the seventies, to calculate throughputs, hardware utilizations and response/turnaround times. The time required to produce a model of an existing system should be less demanding in person effort than that required to produce a simulation model, although that effort should not be underestimated. This approach will give results which are sufficiently accurate for the purposes of capacity planning.

The degrees of accuracy which can and should be sought are:

±5% for hardware utilizations and

±20% for response/turnaround times.

Analytic modelling tools include BGS's BEST/1, ICL's VCMS Modeller, Logica's CAPACITY/Q, Metron's ATHENE and CA's ISS-3.

Criteria for the evaluation of host modelling tools should include the:

* ability of the product to model the hardware and software platform(s) in the organization
* ability of the product to model other hardware and software platforms which may be required in the future
* ability of the software to automate the construction of baseline models directly from monitor data (such software should work at the desired level of granularity; eg transaction type instead of online system)
* ease of use
* comprehensive reporting facilities, eg workload summary level for total utilizations and response times; workload detailed level for breakdown of utilizations, queueing times and response times by device; detailed breakdown of individual devices and I/O paths (utilizations, delays/ queueing times; detailed breakdown of paging/swapping activity)
* ability to model the maximum I/O configuration which is likely to be required (suggested minimum of 120 devices for mainframe systems)
* ability to model the I/O subsystem in detail, ie disk controllers and channels (where they exist), and calculate path delays in addition to device queueing
* ability to model the use of memory directly (not just indirectly via specified attained or maximum multiprogramming levels)
* ability to produce graphs of modelling results
* ability to interface to other software; eg transfer results to a spreadsheet or word processing package

* provision of inbuilt information on hardware characteristics and speeds; eg CPUs, controllers and I/O devices

* ability to facilitate setting up and running, in unattended mode, of models which represent the individual steps of a capacity plan. (For example, it may be required to model the impact of the estimated demand for the next two years on a quarterly basis. Therefore, the plan would have eight steps). It is more productive if the entire plan can be modelled as a single entity without recourse to operator intervention.

7.6 Application sizing tools

In addition to a host modelling tool there may also be a requirement for a complementary product to assist in the sizing of new applications in the development stages before the writing/generation of program code. This is a relatively young marketplace and consequently there are only a limited number of products which are openly available to organizations. The majority of software vendors have such tools but they are typically for vendor use and are therefore not marketed. The available products are most beneficial at the logical or physical design stage. They can be used at earlier stages but the capacity planner must then make assumptions to compensate for the lack of detailed information, accepting the loss of accuracy thus imposed.

Examples of application sizing products include BGS's CRYSTAL (IBM MVS), ICL's VCSR (ICL VME) and Metron's PERSEUS (ICL VME).

Criteria for the evaluation of application sizing tools should include the ability to:

* size an application at all stages of the development lifecycle; ie perform crude through to detailed sizings

* isolate data which relates to the application from the technical details of the hardware and software platforms on which it may run, so that the development team can enter that data in a language which they understand

* cater for a range of transaction frequencies per business function within a single model to cope with any uncertainty; eg minimum, mean and maximum

* cater for a range of possible database accesses per business function within a single model to cope with uncertainty; eg minimum, mean and maximum
* model the proposed application against a range of hardware and software platforms if it is required to compare performance levels and costs (some sizing tools offer a range of predefined hardware models)
* work at a level of detail which is appropriate to the information which is available at the time; eg for an online system it may be desirable to work at the business function, program or message pair level
* size the database, where this is a requirement
* transfer sizing results of proposed application to a host modelling tool to assess its impact on existing applications
* interface to specified development methodologies such as SSADM
* directly interface to CASE tools to extract application details automatically, thus obviating the need for manual input. (Note that this facility does not currently exist. However, it is a natural progression for application sizing tools and will undoubtedly appear in the next two to three years).

Often a selection of tools is necessary because it is rare that a single tool can perform all of the functions outlined.

7.7 Network modelling

For most purposes, PC-based tools are the most appropriate to use, although larger networks may require the use of mainframe-based tools. The four kinds of tool likely to be needed are for trending, queueing theory (also known as analytic modelling), simulation and network pricing.

In addition, systems houses such as PACTEL, Logica and CACI provide modelling consultancy services.

7.7.1 Trend analysis

SAS, a very popular mainframe tool; is now available on PCs as PC/SAS. This provides all of the statistical and reporting features likely to be needed and furthermore is compatible with mainframe SAS for those installations which possess it.

Many spreadsheet packages also now provide statistical analysis and sophisticated display and reporting facilities.

7.7.2 Queueing theory

PC tools are suitable for day-to-day general capacity planning and design of wide-area networks. Features to look out for are user friendliness, speed of data input and execution, geographic and logical network display, data interchange facilities with other packages, production of graphical and numerical reports and the maximum number of nodes the package will handle. Examples include NDS from Logica and NetSolve from I-Net.

Mainframe tools are suitable for design of larger IBM SNA networks. Examples include Best/Net from BGS and NETDA from IBM.

7.7.3 Simulation

Simulation tools may be used for detailed analysis of both wide area and local area network behaviour. They typically run much slower than queueing theory models (hours rather than minutes).

Features to look out for are user friendliness, speed of data input and generation, geographic and logical network display, data interchange facilities with other packages, graphical and numerical reports and the maximum number of nodes the package will handle - much the same as PC tools. Examples include Plexus from Metron and Comnet II/Netsim II from CACI.

7.7.4 Costing

Costing tools may be used for comparing, for example, BT and Mercury costs in addition to performing cost/ performance optimizations in conjunction with a performance analysis/design tool.

Features to look out for are complete tariff data, a complete database of telephone exchanges and a means of keeping this data up to date.

Examples include NDS from Logica, NetworkPrice from VELEC and NetSolve from I-Net.

It is of particular importance in the selection criteria to assess the compatibility of network tools with those selected for the host computer.

8. Bibliography

A Capacity Management Cookbook:
(Logica, 1990).

Capacity Management Primer: Dithmar, Hans;
(CCMS Associates, 1989).

Computer Capacity: A Production Control Approach:
Strauss, Melvin J;
(van Nostrand Reinhold Company, 1981).

Communication Networks Management: Terplan, Kornel;
(Prentice Hall, 1987).

Establishing an IS Management System: Morino, Mario;
(Morino Associates, 1986).

Systems Analysis for Data Transmission: Martin, James;
(Prentice Hall, 1972).

SSADM and Capacity Planning (V3): IS Subject Guide;
(CCTA, 1990).

SSADM and Capacity Planning (V4): IS Subject Guide;
(CCTA, 1991).

Annex A. Glossary of terms

Acronyms used in this module

ATM	Automatic Teller Machines
CAD	Computer Aided Design
CDB	Capacity Management Database
CASE	Computer Assisted Software Engineering
CCITT	Comité Consultatif International Telegraphique et Telephonique
CFIA	Component Failure Impact Analysis
CMIP	Common Management Interface Protocol
CMIS	Common Management Interface Service
CPU	Central Processor Unit
DASD	Direct Access Storage Device
DBMS	Database Management System
EDI	Electronic Data Interchange
EPOS	Electronic Point of Sale
GDN	Government Data Network
GOSIP	Government Open Systems Interface Profile
FM	Facilities Management
ID	Identity (usually terminal id)
I/O	Input/Output
ISO	International Standards Organization
LAN	Local Area Network
MPL	Multi-Programming Level
OCP	Order Code Processor
OR	Operational Requirement
OSI	Open Systems Interconnection
PAD	Package Assembly/Disassembly Device
PRINCE	Projects IN Controlled Environments

PTO	Public Telecommunications Operator
RIRO	Roll In, Roll Out
RPS	Rotational Position Sensing
SLA	Service Level Agreement
SLM	Service Level Manager or Service Level Management
SSADM	Structured Systems Analysis and Design Method
TAP	Total Acquisition Process
TOR	Terms of Reference
TP	Transaction Processing
TPS	Transactions Per Second
TSR	Terminate and Stay Resident (Programs)
UKCMG	UK Computer Measurement Group
VANS	Value Added Network Service
VSI	Virtual Store Interrupt
WAN	Wide Area Network
WORM	Write Once, Read Many (optical disk systems)
3GL	Third Generation (Programming) Language eg COBOL
4GL	Fourth Generation (Programming) Language eg Application Master.

Definitions used in this module

Asynchronous/synchronous
Asynchronous in a communications sense is the ability to transmit each character as a self-contained unit of information, without additional timing information. This method of transmitting data is sometimes called start/stop. Synchronous working involves the use of timing information to allow transmission of data, which is normally done in blocks. Synchronous transmission is usually more efficient than the asynchronous method.

Bridge
A bridge is equiment and techniques used to match circuits to each other ensuring minimum transmission impairment.

Channel
Channel is the physical connection from CPU to an I/O device, usually a controller, or indeed another CPU.

Data transfer time	Data transfer time is the length of time taken for a block or sector of data to be read from or written to an I/O device, such as a disk or tape.
Disk cache controller	Disk cache controllers have memory which is used to store blocks of data which have been read from the disk devices connected to them. If a subsequent I/O requires a record which is still resident in the cache memory, it will be picked up from there, thus saving another physical I/O.
Duplex (full and half)	Full duplex line/channel allows simultaneous transmission in both directions. Half duplex line/channel is capable of transmitting in both directions, but only in one direction at a time.
Echoing	Echoing is a reflection of the transmitted signal from the receiving end, a visual method of error detection in which the signal from the originating device is looped back to that device so that it can be displayed..
Gateway	A gateway is equiment which is used to interface networks so that a terminal on one network can communicate with services or a terminal on another.
Hard fault	Hard faults describe the situation in a virtual memory system when the required page of code or data, which a program was using, has been redeployed by the operating system for some other purpose. This means that another piece of memory must be found to accommodate the code or data, and will involve physical reading/writing of pages to the page file.
Host	A host computer comprises the central hardware and software resources of a computer complex, eg CPU, memory, channels, disk and magnetic tape I/O subsystems plus operating and applications software. The term is used to denote all non-network items.
Latency	Latency describes the elapsed time from the moment when a seek was completed on a disk device to the point when the required data is positioned under the read/write heads. Latency is normally defined by manufacturers as being half the disk rotation time.
Logical I/O	Logical I/O is a read or write request by a program. That request may, or may not, necessitate a physical I/O. For example, on a read request, the required record may already be in a memory buffer and therefore a physical I/O will not be necessary.

Multiplexer	Multiplexers divide data channels into two or more independent fixed data channels of lower speed.
Package assembly/ dissassembly device	A package assembly/disassembly device permits terminals which do not have an interface suitable for direct connection to a packet switched network to access such a network. A PAD converts data to/from packets and handles call set-up and addressing.
Page fault	A program interruption which occurs when a page that is marked 'not in real memory' is referred to by an active page.
Paging	Paging is the I/O necessary to read and write to and from the paging disks: real (not virtual) memory is needed to process data. With insufficient real memory, the operating system writes old pages to disk, and reads new pages from disk, so that the required data and instructions are in real memory.
Percentage utilization	Percentage utilization describes the amount of time that a hardware device is busy over a given period of time. For example, if the CPU is busy for 1800 seconds in a one hour period, its utilization is said to be 50%.
Phantom line error	A phantom line error is a communications error reported by a computer system which is not detected by network monitoring equipment. It is often caused by changes to the circuits and network equipment (eg re-routing circuits at the physical level on a backbone network) while data communications is in progress.
Physical I/O	Physical I/O means that a read or write request from a program has necessitated a physical read or write operation on an I/O device.
Queueing time	Queueing time is incurred when the device, which a program wishes to use, is already busy. The program will therefore have to wait in a queue to obtain service from that device.
Resource cost	This term is used to describe the amount of machine resource that a given task will consume. This resource is usually expressed in seconds for the CPU or the number of I/Os for a disk or tape device.
Resource profile	Resource profile describes the total resource costs which are consumed by an individual online transaction, batch job or program. It is usually expressed in terms of CPU seconds, number of I/Os and memory usage.

Roll in roll out (RIRO)	RIRO is a term which is used on some systems to describe swapping.
Rotational Position Sensing	RPS is a facility which is employed on most mainframes and some minicomputers. When a seek has been initiated the system can free the path from a disc drive to a controller for use by another disc drive, while it is waiting for the required data to come under the read/write heads (latency). This facility usually improves the overall performance of the I/O subsystem.
Seek time	Seek time occurs when the disc read/ write heads are not positioned on the required track. It describes the elapsed time taken to move heads to the right track.
Simulation modelling	Simulation modelling, as the name implies, employs a program which simulates computer processing by describing in detail the path of a job or transaction. It can give extremely accurate results. Unfortunately, it demands a great deal of time and effort from the modeller. It is most beneficial in extremely large or time critical systems where the margin for error is very small.
Soft fault	A soft fault describes the situation in a virtual memory system when the operating system has detected that a page of code or data was due to be reused, ie it is on a list of "free" pages, but it is still actually in memory. It is now rescued and put back into service.
Solid state devices	Solid state disks are memory devices which are made to appear as if they are disk devices. The advantages of such devices are that the service times are much faster than real disks since there is no seek time or latency. The main disadvantage is that they are much more expensive.
Swapping	The reaction of the operating system to insufficient real memory: swapping occurs when too many tasks are perceived to be competing for limited resources. It is the physical movement of an entire task (eg all real memory pages of an address space may be moved at one time from main storage to auxiliary storage).
Terminal emulation	Terminal emulation is achieved by software running on an intelligent device, typically a PC or workstation, which allows that device to function as an interactive terminal connected to a host system. Examples of such emulation software includes IBM 3270 BSC or SNA, ICL C03, or Digital VT100.
Terminal I/O	Terminal I/O is a read from, or a write to, an online device such as a VDU or remote printer.

Thrashing	A condition in a virtual storage system where an excessive proportion of CPU time is spent moving data between main and auxiliary storage.
Tree structures	In data structures, a series of connected nodes without cycles. One node is termed the root and is the starting point of all paths, other nodes termed leaves terminate the paths. It can be used to represent hierarchical structures.
Virtual memory system	Virtual memory systems were developed to increase the size of memory by adding an auxiliary storage layer which resides on disk.
VSI	VSI (virtual storage interrupt) is an ICL VME term for a page fault.
WORM	WORM or CD-WORM is the term which is frequently used to describe optical read only disks, standing for Write Once Read Many.
Workloads	Workloads in the context of Capacity Management Modelling, are a set of forecasts which detail the estimated resource usage over agreed planning horizons. Workloads generally represent discrete business applications and can be further sub-divided into types of work (interactive, timesharing, batch).

Annex B. Monitors

This annex describes the types of monitors which are typically available and the information which is collected by them. The list of data items which is given below under each type of monitor is intended to reflect the minimum which should be expected and it is, by no means a definitive list. Reporting requirements are not addressed. Any monitor should be thoroughly evaluated for its suitability to local needs before it is chosen and subsequently implemented.

B.1 System monitors

This type of monitor, sometimes referred to as a time-driven monitor, provides information on performance from an overall system and sub-grouping (workload) viewpoint. Examples of sub-grouping include virtual machine (IBM VM); performance group (IBM MVS); policy (ICL); or individual process/task (DEC VMS, Data General, Wang, NCR, Stratus, Tandem etc).

The monitors collect data items on a sampling basis at predefined time intervals which may be user-definable. The various items are then written to the monitor file at a user-defined interval, eg every 10 minutes.

Overall system metrics should include:

* CPU idle time
* total CPU utilization. Beware of the difference between total measured CPU and the true total CPU usage. Some monitors cannot measure certain usage, such as I/O interrupt handling. They overcome this problem by subtracting percentage idle time from 100%
* I/O subsystem:
    - channel utilization (where applicable)
    - controller utilization
    - for each device:
        · I/O rates per second or total number of I/Os
        · average queue length
        · device busy utilization
        · average service time for one I/O (excluding queueing time)

* Virtual Memory system:
    - total paging (VSI) rate
    - total swapping (RIRO) rate
    - total physical paging (VSI) I/Os
    - total swapping (RIRO) I/Os.

Sub-grouping items should include:

* total measured CPU
* total number of physical I/Os
* total paging (VSI) rate
* total swapping (RIRO) rate
* average main memory occupancy.

B.2 Accounting

This term is synonymous with "Event Driven Monitors". Data is recorded when certain events occur: eg logon; logoff; program, task, or process termination; job termination; allocation or deletion of disk space.

The data items which are logged should include:

* job, process, task or program name
* start and finish times or time of the event
* total measured CPU (termination records)
* total number of physical I/Os (termination records)
* average (and maximum) main memory occupancy (termination records)
* paging (VSI) rate (termination records)
* swapping (RIRO) rate (termination records)
* amount of disk space allocated/deleted
* I/O by device (termination records, only available on certain systems).

B.3 Transaction processing monitors

Transaction processing monitoring software provides a basic framework which is used to simplify and quicken the development process for online systems. They obviate the need to write specific code to deal with items such as: security of access; screen handling; multi-phase transactions; message routeing; logging; and recovery.

Examples of TP monitors include IMS/DC (IBM), CICS (IBM) and TPMS (ICL). Data which relates to the performance of TP monitors is usually provided by the vendor and in some cases software supplied by third-parties.

Two main types of record are written, at system level (normally at system closedown, but some monitors also provide information at predefined intervals of time eg hourly intervals) and at individual transaction level.

System level statistics should include:

* name of the TP system
* start-up and close-down times
* total number of transactions executed
* total measured CPU time used
* total number of physical I/Os (preferably by device)
* average (minimum and maximum) main memory occupancy
* total paging (VSI) rate
* total swapping (RIRO) rate.

Task/transaction level statistics should include:

* transaction, task or program name
* measured CPU time
* number of physical I/Os
* average main memory occupancy
* paging (VSI) rate
* swapping (RIRO) rate
* response time (host).

B.4 DBMS statistics

When a DBMS is employed, some systems allocate the DBMS resources which have been consumed to the DBMS itself, rather than to the transaction which was responsible for it.

System level statistics should include:

* name of the DBMS
* start-up and closedown times
* total number of tasks or transactions executed
* total measured CPU time used
* total number of database calls
* total number of logical I/Os or rows accessed for relational databases
* number of rows returned (relational DBMS only)
* total number of physical I/Os (preferably by device)
* buffer usage
* number of inserts, updates and deletes
* number of physical records accessed (eg cascade deletions of associated records)
* overflow statistics
* average (minimum and maximum) main memory occupancy
* total paging (VSI) rate
* total swapping (RIRO) rate.

Task/transaction level statistics should include:

* transaction/task/program name
* measured CPU time
* number of logical I/Os or rows accessed (relational DBMS only)
* number of physical records accessed (eg cascade deletions of associated records)
* number of physical I/Os
* average main memory occupancy
* paging (VSI) rate
* swapping (RIRO) rate.

B.5 Network statistics

This section lists typical items which can be collected from some host-resident network monitors.

Data is normally collected on a user specified time interval basis, eg every 15 minutes.

Example of items for a line or controller:

* line or controller network identifier/ name
* total messages sent
* total messages received
* total bytes sent
* total bytes received
* number of polls
* number of messages retransmitted
* number of bytes retransmitted
* utilization of line/controller.

Examples of items for a specified network name:

* network name (eg terminal id)
* number of input messages
* number of output messages
* average size of input message
* average size of output message
* average response time
* number of transactions with a response time less than n1, n2, n3 ... seconds (where n1, n2, n3 ... may be specified by the user). The number of target response time bins to hold this type of information may vary)
* number of messages retransmitted.

Note that response times may be for the network only, for the sum of host and network, or for host and network separately.

Annex C. Performance management and the CDB

Sections 3 and 4 of this module in particular, stress the importance of performance management in relation to capacity management. The practice of performance management is simplified when a capacity management database containing appropriate information is available. In similar fashion to the earlier sections of this module, guidance about mainframes and networks has been separated.

C.1 Mainframe (host) investigations

Investigations should centre upon:

* a software review which examines the availability and functionality of
    - all technical monitors, including system (time driven), accounting (event driven), TP and DBMS
    - the software tools which are necessary to manipulate and store the monitor data (including the CDB)
    - performance modelling tools (to facilitate service management)
    - ancillary software, eg word processing, reporting and graphics
    - trend information
* details of current hardware and software products in the organization, plus any proposed changes
* details of any contingency plans
* the identification and preliminary understanding of all existing applications
* details of all proposed new application developments
* the identification of all applications
* the identification of any current performance problems
* any existing reports or plans which appertain to capacity management eg workload usage, utilizations, trends
* any other information which is deemed to be appropriate.

C.1.1 Mainframe performance management

The items which should be monitored include:

* on-line response times
* workloads
* batch turnaround times
* utilizations of all major hardware components; eg CPU, channels, controllers and devices
* the use of memory, including paging and swapping rates
* software locking.

C.1.2 Exception reporting

The recommended, primary method of monitoring is via the use of daily exception reporting (ie a report which identifies the breaching of a predefined performance threshold such as response time). This type of reporting reduces the amount of technical data which is usually captured, to a summary level. Summary reports quickly highlight when individual hardware or software thresholds are close to being or have actually been exceeded. Products which provide an exception reporting capability, in real-time and/or batch mode, are available on certain operating environments (see section 7). If a product is not available it is usually cost-effective to develop an in-house system that will subsequently save the manual effort that is otherwise required to inspect and reduce the data. An example of an exception report is given in Figure C.1.

Figure C1: Performance exception report

Performance Exception Report - 3/2/90

Time	Item	Threshold Util (%)	Actual Util (%)
1045	CPU	70	91
1100	CPU	70	88
1115	CPU	70	92
1115	Disk Cntrlr 1	30	42
1115	Disk D140	40	47
1115	Disk D142	40	51
1115	Disk D147	40	50
1200	Disk Cntrlr 1	30	32

Exception reports highlighting problems must be acted upon quickly. It will be necessary to inform the help desk and to complete an incident report. It is essential to take action to clear performance problems before service level objectives have been compromised.

The following list provides a starter set of thresholds for hardware utilizations which can be employed in any automated or manual exception reporting system. It should be amended where necessary to suit individual organizations, based on experience or any alternative, recommended figures for a particular hardware and/or software platform:

* CPU utilization for system tasks and interactive work should not exceed 70%
* CPU utilization may exceed 70% and reach 90+% only if the residual work is batch and the degraded turnaround times for that residual work are acceptable
* disk device utilizations should not exceed 30% to ensure fast response times for interactive work (higher utilizations, 50-60%, may be acceptable for devices which are dedicated to batch work)
* disk devices which contain paging or swapping files should not exceed 30% utilization
* disk service time (seek time, plus latency, plus data transfer time) should not exceed 30 milliseconds on non-cached disk devices (note that some older disks (pre-1985) may have service times in the region of 35-40 milliseconds)
* disk service times for cached disks should be less than 10 milliseconds (the actual figure will depend upon the hit ratio - the percentage of I/Os which can utilize the cache instead of performing a physical I/O on the disk itself - and the size of the I/O)
* hit read ratios on disk cache controllers should exceed 90% for interactive work and 65% for batch work
* service times for solid state devices (RAM disks) should typically be less than 5 milliseconds, depending on the size of the block(s) being transferred, the overhead for a single I/O (in lieu of seek time and latency) should be less than 1 millisecond

* disk controller utilizations should not exceed 40% for interactive work where RPS (Rotational Position Sensing) is employed, or 25% if non-RPS
* disk channel utilizations (where applicable) should not normally exceed 30%
* tape channel utilizations should not exceed 60%
* recommended page fault or swapping rates should be obtained from the manufacturer (it is not possible to provide a 'rule of thumb' figure since the rate will depend upon the speed of the processor and the operating system).

In addition to information on hardware thresholds, data is also required on any failure to meet service level agreements.

C.1.3 Monitoring/tuning

Investigate all failures to provide the agreed service levels or any regular instances of the hardware thresholds being exceeded. Obtain the data for such investigations from standard, detailed performance reports which are provided by the hardware manufacturers or third-party software vendors' tools. In addition, employ real-time monitors, where appropriate, if they are available, since they provide more detailed information.

Failure to meet service levels is caused by one or more bottlenecks within the system, - assuming the service levels were wisely chosen in the first instance - as discussed in the following paragraphs.

CPU bottlenecks

CPU bottlenecks can be caused by any one (or more) of the following reasons.

Volume of work

The number of transactions or jobs is too large to be supported on the current processor(s). If this is a temporary situation it may be acceptable to endure the degraded service levels. It may be necessary to reduce the demand by limiting the number of concurrent online users or batch streams. This will also give rise to degraded service, albeit for a smaller number of users. Another option is to see if any work can be moved from this peak period to a time when the CPU is more lightly used, eg batch work can be run off-peak. Clearly the Service Level Manager needs to be involved if users are to be convinced that off-peak working is viable and necessary.

Excessive CPU usage

If the amount of CPU consumed by individual transaction types or jobs is excessive the usual causes are that:

* the usage of the transaction has increased, or
* amendments have been made to the functionality of an application. In the latter case, arrange to investigate the application code to check for any obvious inefficiencies and to see if any redesign, usually in the area of database navigation, is necessary. Carry out this work in close liaison with application development or support. Redesign of the application may involve a great deal of work. Therefore, assess the effort against the expected benefits before commencement of the work.

Excessive loading into memory of programs for online transactions

Alleviate the problem by ensuring that frequently used programs are kept resident in memory.

Frequent spawning of sub-processes on minicomputers

Minimize or totally avoid this wherever possible as it incurs a heavy overhead. Redesign of the application is usually the only cure.

Excessive system overheads

The most common cause of this situation is "thrashing". This is a term used to describe the condition when memory management systems encounter a severe shortage of memory and spend more time paging and swapping than doing real work. (See memory bottlenecks). This situation can usually only be alleviated by restricting the amount of work which is run concurrently, thus decreasing the competition for memory resources - or by purchasing more memory.

I/O bottlenecks

I/O bottlenecks can occur at channel, controller or device level. Solutions include:

* minimize the amount of physical I/O by the effective use of memory buffers, or cache disk controllers (where present), or by increasing block sizes where access is typically sequential
* balance the overall I/O load by moving files from the offending device, controller and channel to a lightly-loaded part of the I/O subsystem

* reconfigure the I/O subsystem by
  - moving any hardware which is causing the problem; a number of disks which are leading to a high controller utilization could be moved to another, less used, controller
  - provide another controller which the problem disks can use, thus providing two paths instead of one (this assumes that the operating system can make use of alternative paths. Some systems may only use alternative paths if the primary path is not functioning; ie they provide resilience)
* spread paging and swapping files over multiple disks (a common problem, particularly on minicomputers, is to find that all such files have been placed on the systems disk, thus causing a bottleneck)
* lessen I/Os due to program loading by keeping frequently used programs resident in memory
* reduce high disk service times by
  - keeping seek times to a minimum: if two files on the same disk are being accessed frequently, they should be physically positioned as close together as possible on the disk to minimize head movement. If this is not possible move one of the files to another disk to overcome the problem
  - decreasing the data transfer time by reducing the block size and/or the number of blocks which are transferred (be aware that this action may well generate additional I/Os, and possibly exacerbate the situation).

Memory bottlenecks

Memory bottlenecks are caused by excessive demands for memory from the total workload. Excessive demand leads to increased paging/swapping which, in turn, consumes more CPU resources and generates more paging and swapping I/Os. The degradation to the service typically increases exponentially with any additional pressure on memory, ultimately leading to 'thrashing'. Memory bottlenecks can cause much greater problems than the CPU or I/O subsystem, and can exacerbate CPU and I/O problems. Attempt to resolve the problem by:

* reducing the amount of concurrent work which is competing for memory

* reducing the working set sizes of any processes which use large amounts of memory, where this is appropriate. (Some experimentation will be required to obtain the optimum size for a process which involves not using too much memory, while at the same time keeping the number of page faults to an acceptable level).

Software bottlenecks

Software bottlenecks are typically caused by locks which are placed on resources; eg a database page, by an individual task while it is using those resources. While the lock is in place no other task can use that resource. This can lead to unacceptable delays which may endanger service levels. The usual reason for a lock is to maintain the integrity of the system.

These locks, (enqueues, or conflicts as they are otherwise known) are found in operating software, most typically database management systems and TP monitors. Information on the amount of locking, and possibly the total delay, may be found in the DBMS or TP Monitor statistics. Unfortunately, statistics tend only to provide summary level information relating to the whole day and therefore fail to provide sufficiently detailed information for the investigator.

Find out precisely what information is provided by the monitor(s) which are installed. In some cases, it may only be possible to discover a locking problem by a process of elimination; eg if a response time is greater than the sum of waiting for an available process, service time and queueing time.

Encourage discipline in the use of locks at the right level (page, record, ...) ie use lowest level which still maintains integrity. Attempt to delay locking until updating, but be aware that this might mean that more records may have to be re-read.

If the delays due to locking are unacceptable it will be necessary to check the application to discover if:

* the lock is absolutely necessary, and

* it is set at the appropriate level; eg is the lock at the database area or table level when it only needs to be at page, record or row level?

* there are any other methods of minimizing the effects of the locking; eg by altering the design of the application.

This work needs to be performed in close liaison with application development or support staff.

Other response time problems can be caused by:

* multi-tasking or concurrency levels set too low
* dispatching priority.

System parameter settings

Degraded response times or batch turnaround times can be caused by the concurrency level being set too low. The concurrency level is the number of tasks which are utilized by the application in order to use CPU, I/O and memory resources. If the concurrency level has been reached, any additional task which arrives is queued until one of the resident tasks has completed its processing. Try increasing the concurrency level. Monitor any change closely to check for any possible side-effects. Increased concurrency may cause CPU, I/O or memory bottlenecks which may exacerbate rather than improve the situation.

Poor response times can also be caused by injudicious settings of dispatching or scheduling priorities. For example, a low dispatching priority may have an impact on response time, but only if the use of CPU resources for the offending transactions is high (50+% of the total service time) and the overall CPU utilization of the machine is 60+%. It is important to remember that the raising of priority for one workload will have a deleterious effect on any other workloads whose priorities have effectively been lowered. Therefore, it is important to monitor closely the impact of a change on all workloads.

It is possible on some systems to limit the amount of resources which are consumed when a transaction is being serviced to prevent it from using more than a fair share of the system. Experiment to obtain optimum settings so that all workloads receive the appropriate level of service. Again, the performance improvement of one workload can result in a detrimental effect on another workload.

All changes which are proposed by performance management for the improvement of the system must be approved by the change management process.

Performance monitoring and tuning should not be limited to past and present. The Capacity Manager should look ahead, trying to predict the eventual impact of any problems which currently may be minor, but which may become major, threatening service levels. The use of a host modelling tool to predict future performance may be beneficial in this process. The modelling tool is also useful in predicting the effect of tuning changes prior to actual implementation.

C.2 Network investigations

Network investigations have parallels with investigations into computer systems, but have additional features and a somewhat different emphasis. The differences arise from the importance of topographical information (ie where items of network equipment are physically placed and how they are physically joined together) and the dependence for service on third-party suppliers, such as the Public Telecommunications Operator (PTO). The objective is to scope the amount of work to be done in order to assess the resources required to do it. The individual activities are as follows:

* gather information on the size of network required - at this stage restrict the information to:
    - the number and sites of geographic locations served by the network
    - the numbers of terminals at each of these sites
    - the applications and services delivered and their criticality to these sites, as defined by service level agreements or, in their absence, by stated user requirements
    - planned changes (eg relocations)
* gather information on the technology used in the network - in particular:
    - what facilities are available for network performance monitoring, both on the computer system and on the network itself
    - what communications technologies and protocols are used as the basis of the network architecture, eg X.25
    - what network performance statistics are currently gathered, and what happens to them
    - what procedures and tools currently exist within the organization to assist with planning network changes

* identify who is responsible for the network; specifically, whether it belongs to the organization or whether it is a third-party service, such as a Value-Added Network Service or the Government Data Network (GDN)
* establish who to contact to obtain definitive answers about:
    - detailed application information, to calculate traffic demand
    - (for private networks) detailed network topology information, to plan connectivity changes and avoid performance degradation
    - (for private networks) detailed circuit information, to isolate potential problems and plan the required degree of resilience
    - detailed network costing information, to establish the most cost-effective service for users
    - detailed performance characteristics of network equipment (for private networks) and equipment attached to the network, to calculate response times and throughputs.

The answers to these questions will reveal the specific tools and skills needed to carry out effective network capacity management, and how much work needs to be done to satisfy the demand for maintainable levels of service.

The items which should be monitored include:

* interactive application response times as perceived by end users and by the monitoring software
* file transfer transmission times
* utilizations of all circuits and major network hardware items
* circuit error rates
* call durations on dialled lines
* traffic rates and session durations on public networks.

C.2.1 Exception reporting

Use the same methods as described for the host computer. Performance data is normally captured on the host computer directly and/or on specialist network management equipment. This data needs to be consolidated and processed on the host computer to produce exception reports.

The following list provides a starter set of exception thresholds. These are 'rules of thumb' and should be modified in the light of experience, suppliers' performance criteria and modelling/measurement results to suit a particular network:

* total bi-directional utilization on a half duplex link should not exceed 70%
* unidirectional utilization on a full duplex link should not exceed 90%
* multiplexer and packet switch utilizations should not exceed 40% of their throughput capacity
* front-end processor utilization should not exceed 85-90% of its throughput capacity at network startup time and at other times, its utilization should not exceed 40%
* local area network transmission media utilization should not exceed 50%
* dial-up line utilization should not exceed one hour per week per remote location.

Figures for maximum recommended buffer utilizations in packet switches, multiplexers and front end processors must be obtained from the manufacturers concerned. There are no safe 'rules of thumb' because of internal architectural variations.

C.2.2 Monitoring/tuning

Monitoring and tuning follows the same pattern as described for host computer monitoring. Failure to meet service levels is caused by one or more bottlenecks, discussed in the following paragraphs.

Line bottlenecks

Line bottlenecks can be caused by one or more of the following:

Message profiles

It is important to know in an interactive environment how much of the screen is refreshed by data transmitted. For example, if the whole of an 80-column x 25 row screen is retransmitted, this implies 2,000 characters. If this is transmitted in 256-byte packets, where 240 bytes are data (the rest being protocol overheads) this represents 9 packets in all, ie 2,304 bytes.

On a 9600 bps line with 70% utilization (using the rule of thumb mentioned earlier) this represents a minimum transmission time from the computer to the terminal of 2.74 seconds. The response time perceived by the user is worse than this, owing to transmission queueing delays and the host computer response time. This basic 2.74 second overhead can only be reduced by changing the applications design or the system software to reduce the amount of refreshed data, or improving line specification.

Line error rates

Line errors tend to occur in bursts. The effect is to cause real data retransmission or interference in the protocol flow. The former is less disruptive, since it will be trapped by the protocol. Interference with the protocol flow can cause disruption of several seconds while the protocol is re-established. The effect of line error therefore increases the variability of response times to the user. If the measured host computer response times are constant yet the user response times are variable, this is often an indication of line errors.

Traffic priorities

Where several applications share the same communications line it is important to set file transfer, electronic mail and graphics data at a lower transmission priority than that used for normal interactive transaction processing traffic. This is because the former tends to transmit long blocks with zero think time, ie requests to transmit the next block are constantly queued. The effect is to cause line congestion and poor interactive response times. The priority order, from highest to lowest, should be:

* short fixed-length messages (eg ATM, EPOS)
* short variable-length messages (eg interactive transactions)

* longer messages (eg EMAIL, TELEX)
* heavy screen-based data (eg Graphics, CAD)
* light file transfer (eg EDI)
* medium file transfer (eg standard data files)
* heavy file transfer (eg Graphics, CAD).

If necessary, route this traffic over separate, parallel circuits to achieve the required response times and throughput. It is undesirable to mix EPOS and heavy file transfer traffic on the same links since the long transmission blocks used by the latter will inevitably cause delays to the high-priority traffic and increase response time variability.

Physical circuit rerouteing

Many wide area networks consist of a logical and a physical layer. The logical link between, let us say, two packet switches may be physically achieved by one or more circuits linked in series through time-division multiplexers. Although satisfactory for voice traffic, if more than three circuits are joined in this way to form a logical link, the error rates experienced can be unacceptably high for data transmission. Often this circuit switching and linking is performed by equipment managed by voice telecommunications staff, having no means of knowing the traffic that is travelling on the individual circuits. It is essential to set up permanent liaison between voice and data network operations and management staff. Ideally the equipment used for network management by the two groups should be linked. Otherwise, problems known as phantom line errors may arise.

Node bottlenecks

Node bottlenecks can be caused by one or more of the following:

Shortage of buffers

This is caused by too much inbound traffic with which the switch or multiplexer needs to cope. This will cause response time delays and reduce throughput. The solution is either to bypass the node or to increase the capacity of its output links. Adding more buffer capacity merely postpones the problem.

Shortage of CPU power

This is serious and can cause message loss and/or corruption. The solution is either to upgrade the hardware or to bypass the node.

Shortage of throughput capacity

This can be serious, but can often be rectified by software upgrade and/or tuning according to the suppliers' advice. Otherwise, bypass the node or have its hardware upgraded.

Route bottlenecks

Route bottlenecks (ie network end-to-end delays) are caused by one or more of the following:

Topology design
(ie poor physical topology design or traffic routeing)

This creates node or link bottlenecks in the end-to-end traffic paths. The solution for this is to realign circuits and routes using a modelling tool to optimize the traffic flows and circuit costs.

Routeing software
(ie poor routeing software in the nodal switches)

As with manual routeing designs, the solution is often to realign the network using a modelling tool. Frequently, a single extra bypass circuit to ease the route concerned is all that is required.

NOTE:

Remember that every route or path through the network is made up of links and nodes. Thus an individual link or node problem may be a symptom of a larger routeing problem.

LAN bottlenecks

LAN bottlenecks are caused by one or more of the following:

File server queueing

This is disk queueing and thus a computer rather than a network problem, and should be dealt with as such - additional computing power may be required. The use of an individual user's PC as a shared file server is not recommended since the user's work can interfere with the shared service.

Gateway problem

Wide area networks typically run at much lower transmission speeds than LANs, measured in kilobits rather than megabits per second. Customer expectations must match these power line speeds. If the gateway is also a file server, the operating software may cause the file server traffic to produce gateway queues - and vice versa. It is therefore strongly recommended that PC file servers are not used as gateways. Specialist multi-tasking hardware and software as found in a minicomputer is however appropriate to this dual role.

Bridge problem

Bridges are often speed-constrained like gateways. The solution is to minimize the traffic across bridges by using filter bridges or by physically re-grouping LAN equipment.

NB: LAN problems are seldom caused by transmission bottlenecks on the LAN itself, because of the high bandwidth employed. In practice, the transmission utilization of most LANs is under 10%.

Response times

Response times need very careful consideration both when tuning, and at the design stage, because they relate to human expectations. Consistency of response time is much more important than a good average response time. This is because of the effect of response times on manual working patterns. Humans can adjust to slower response times by carrying out parallel activities, so long as response times are consistent. It is variations in response times which cause broken work patterns and dissatisfied customers.

For example, a customer will find a response time of 3 seconds, plus or minus 2 seconds, much more disagreeable than one of 4 seconds, plus or minus 1 second. This tends to bear out the theory that good, consistent response times improve productivity, since the worst response time (5 seconds) remains the same. Furthermore, tuning the system to reduce response time to the lower figure may not only increase variability but may use more resources and disrupt other services. For this reason, the statistics monitored and gathered should include not only the mean response times but also the variances or 95th percentiles of the response times.

Protocol bottlenecks

Protocol bottlenecks are generally caused by insufficient account being taken of protocol overheads in planning response times.

It is important to define exactly what response times mean for various protocols, otherwise misunderstandings will arise not only in Service Level Agreements but also with suppliers.

The following definition for response time is strongly recommended:

The response time should be taken as the time from the transmission of the last character of an input message being entered by the user, to the receipt of the last character of the corresponding output message.

Each type of communications protocol has its own implications on performance as a result of this definition.

Half duplex

For half duplex synchronous protocols, as used by terminals such as ICL DRS and IBM 3270, the response time is the time between the user pressing SEND or ENTER and the keyboard unlocking to accept another SEND or ENTER following receipt of a response. When estimating inbound and outbound message sizes, it is important to include non-displayed attribute bytes (such as high/low intensity, field position, colour, etc). It is also important to know whether the terminal protocol transmits:

* altered characters on a screen
* the entire screen refreshed by each message
* some intermediate data set.

In addition, there will be protocol overheads associated with terminal polls and responses which generate extra traffic (and thus line utilization). The use of network monitors will be invaluable in establishing a true profile of the network traffic.

Full duplex

For full duplex asynchronous protocols, as used by terminals such as DEC VT100, the situation is more complex, depending on the character echoing technique being used. For example if the echoing is:

* performed by the terminal itself, the communications traffic may be assessed as being broadly similar to the half-duplex synchronous case
* performed by a local multiplexor or X.25 PAD, there will be extra traffic on the link between the PAD or multiplexer, but not over the rest of the network. Such extra output traffic will overlap with input traffic on what is a dedicated terminal line and will not cause a network bottleneck
* carried out by the distant computer, then the echo traffic will be carried across the network and must be taken into account in the aggregate traffic on multiplexed links.

Remember also that with asynchronous traffic every key depression (including cursor key use) causes a character to be sent over the network to the computer. These must be included in traffic estimates. However, for most standard asynchronous protocols there will be no equivalent to the synchronous poll/response traffic.

To illustrate the difference between the case of an asynchronous full duplex computer-echo system and a synchronous half duplex system, consider the following example.

Input message length = Input characters

Output message length = Output characters

Assume for the sake of simplicity that the control characters are the same in both cases, very much simplified protocols are used in the two cases (in which the block overhead for synchronous transmission equates to the byte overhead for asynchronous transmission), and there is no queueing.

Synchronous Case:

Total inbound traffic = input data characters + poll response characters

Total outbound traffic = output data characters + poll characters

Response time = line time to transmit input data characters + host response time + poll/response time + line time to transmit output data characters.

Asynchronous Case:

Total inbound traffic = input data characters

Total outbound traffic = input data characters + output data characters

Response time = line time to transmit the last input data character + host response time + line time to transmit output data characters.

The full duplex nature of asynchronous traffic also permits data to be typed in ahead of the computer being able to process it. It is frequently the case that the end-user perceives the response time for asynchronous services to be better than for synchronous. However, this is achieved at a cost in terms of line utilization because of the echoed input data. Therefore bottlenecks arise more quickly on lines carrying asynchronous traffic.

Asynchronous traffic passed through statistical multiplexers is subject to a further bottleneck caused by multiplexer overloading. Careful monitoring of multiplexer loadings in conjunction with the use of modelling tools is essential if the creation of these bottlenecks is to be anticipated and avoided.

Poor file transfer throughput is another frequent instance of a protocol bottleneck. Many systems use terminal emulation for file transfer. This implies using a half duplex protocol. As a result, there is a fixed time gap between transmitted blocks, roughly equal to the poll/response time. Increasing the line speed does not improve performance; it simply increases the proportion of the total time spent in polling and responding. The answer in this case is to increase the transmitted block size substantially to increase the line utilization. However, the use of terminal emulation may limit the maximum file transfer block size to around 2 Kbytes: adequate on a 9.6 Kbps line, but very inefficient on a 64 Kbps line. Furthermore, if there are other applications sharing the line, the transmission time of long file transfer blocks may have a serious impact on the response times of the other applications.

If, as a result of monitoring, circuit changes are deemed necessary, the change control procedure should ensure that the voice telecommunications staff are informed in order to coordinate procurement, if appropriate, from the circuit provider.

C.3 Capacity Management Database

A Capacity Management Database (CDB) is the cornerstone of a successful performance management system. It is a repository which contains technical, business and ancillary data items. This information is used to form the basis of much performance and capacity management work, including the formulation of reports.

The main tasks are to design, build, maintain and implement the CDB and produce a regular set of management reports.

Reporting, in this context, refers to past and present performance. Reports produced in other phases of capacity management (forecasts and plans) are covered in the appropriate section.

Note that the term CDB is a generic term which in the context of this publication is used to indicate a means of storing relevant data. In reality, the data requirements of host and network capacity management are different and they may be implemented as discrete databases. (See also 3.1.6.3 regarding the concept of a single all-encompassing database). The actual requirements of each part are described in the following sub-sections.

Decide first the precise nature of the CDB. Should it:

* be entirely custom built?
* rely solely on files which are produced by the monitor products?
* be a mix of the above (the more likely approach)?

Consider where the data should reside; either on the host, a PC or both. The sheer volume of detailed data items will probably dictate storing them on the host. However, it is possible to keep summarized data on a PC, if required. It is recommended that a housekeeping schedule is employed to minimize the volume of data maintained: keep summaries wherever possible.

It should be noted that building the CDB is likely to be the most labour intensive of all capacity management activities, it may consume 30-40% of the total effort which is required to implement capacity management.

C.3.1 Mainframe CDB

The technical items in the CDB depend on the information which can be obtained from the various monitors which are installed, but typically includes:

* CPU utilization, total and by major workload
* memory usage and paging/swapping rates, total and by major workload
* I/O utilization, total, by device and by major workload
* channel and controller utilizations
* job and optionally job step data including elapsed times, CPU usage, number of I/Os, memory usage and page/swap rates, number of print lines
* transaction rates by major workload and by transaction type

* average resource usage (CPU, I/Os and memory) by major transaction or job type - termed resource profiles (see Annex D, Workload Management).

The amount of disk space which is available for a CDB dictates the amount of detailed information which can be kept online. Keep detailed information for one week. Note that transaction level detail (TP Monitor statistics) may need to be kept on magnetic tape since the volume of detail is likely to be prohibitively large. Aim to keep summary level data items for all system wide and workload metrics for each hour of every day for as long as possible; eg two or more years. Detailed job information should be kept for as long as required by cost management.

In addition to the technical data, it is important to relate those resources which are being consumed against business metrics:

* number of accounts which are supported
* number of clients that the organization deals with
* number of staff on the payroll, personnel or pension system
* number of branches
* number of terminals and so on.

It is therefore necessary to elicit business metrics which may drive the individual workloads and keep this information in the CDB. The information is used for workload forecasting and for making sense of what it is that you are monitoring! Having identified the business metrics, it may be possible to obtain the data directly by accessing the relevant application files and storing it in the CDB. Alternatively, it may be necessary to extract the data manually from control reports and key it into the CDB. One observation per business or business type should be stored per week, month or quarter as appropriate.

Also store in the CDB ancillary items which are required by capacity management. Examples include:

* hardware utilization thresholds
* service level requirements, from SLAs
* the results of workload forecasting exercises.

It is important to maintain the integrity of the CDB; it is recommended that one person is appointed to be responsible for updating the database where necessary and that, in general, other staff are restricted to read only access. Any updating must be undertaken with the agreement of the configuration manager.

It is vital that comprehensive operating instructions are available for all regular performance management jobs which are run as batch jobs, eg daily (create detail for that day), weekly (detail merges or summary creation/updates), and weekly or monthly reports. Make recovery instructions available to cater for jobs which fail to complete. The target should be to automate this work as much as possible.

C.3.2 Network Database

Since network capacity management is primarily about measurement, it is essential to find out how much traffic is flowing through the network, what the network is physically capable of transmitting and to where. This information is held in the Network Database and is used to build a model to determine the maximum throughput capacity of the network for each application. It is the correlation of the information within this database which provides the basis for successful capacity management.

The central Network Database or Configuration Management Database(CMDB) holds an inventory of all items of network equipment, where they are located, their performance criteria, costing information, application message sizes and transaction volumes, application performance requirements and a history log of performance statistics.

The Network Database corresponds to the performance database used for host computer capacity management (CDB), but tends to be rather more complex since it includes geographic and circuit costing information in addition to performance statistics, service level data and technical equipment criteria. Its use is also not restricted to Capacity Managers. Subsets of the information are used in all areas of network management, for example for voice and data network installation planning, configuration management, performance analysis, help desk information and billing. Because of its shared use, it is recommended that the responsibility for maintaining this database be given to a custodian independent of other network management functions. See also 3.3.4.

The procedure to build up the contents of this database comprises four tasks.

Firstly

Determine which applications are delivered over the network, and to where and from where they are delivered. For existing applications on private networks, it is also helpful to know the route taken by this traffic across the network. Obtain this information from the business analysts responsible for the applications and/or from Network Operations.

Secondly

Obtain quantitative details of these applications. These are needed to calculate traffic volumes, therefore the information required for each application includes:

* average message lengths in each direction
* average number of message pairs per business transaction
* average number of transactions from each site at peak times
* times of peaks
* average host response times per message
* envisaged traffic growth over the next planning periods (these are normally one year intervals, but there is no hard and fast rule about this)
* communications protocol overheads (specifically, this must include polling message overheads and transmission block size, header and trailer lengths).

File transfer may be treated in similar fashion, although an additional constraint such as a specified overall transmission time may need to be ascertained. In the case of file transfer, the average message length is normally taken as the data block size and the average number of message pairs per business transaction is equivalent to what is often termed the 'success unit': the maximum number of data blocks which need to be retransmitted if an error occurs in one of them. Take care with file transfer in determining how successful or unsuccessful receipt of data is acknowledged. If done by a message sent at the application (rather than the protocol) layer, then there exists a true applications message pair to which protocol overheads need to be added. If done at the protocol layer only, then the data transfer may be treated as effectively unidirectional. In practice, most file transfer systems do have an applications-level acknowledgement, but this must be checked.

Glean the above traffic information from the applications designer, the business analyst, the communications systems programmer and from performance statistics gathered in the Network Database.

Where an applications package is being used, measured (built-in) performance statistics are invaluable in establishing average message lengths and numbers of message pairs. Otherwise, some analysis of the package is needed by a systems analyst to estimate these figures. Remember that this type of task is prone to error. Note that at first the custodian of the Network Database may not be collecting sufficient or appropriate statistics for capacity management purposes. It is the responsibility of the Network Capacity Manager to specify the data collection requirements.

It is unrealistic to gather statistics on all applications, from all locations, all of the time, because of the sheer volume of data concerned. Selectivity is called for to reduce the data to manageable proportions. The recommended approach is to gather data for 80% (approximately) of the traffic from each site, making sure that high-priority traffic is included. This typically produces an application profile of some six or eight applications to be dealt with individually. Group together the remainder of the traffic as a general application and deal with it as a whole.

Break down the traffic in the manner defined in the foregoing. Gross traffic levels, as typically provided by line monitoring equipment and packet switches, are of little use for capacity management purposes, since these figures do not permit traffic to be readily separated into streams of high and low user priority. Indeed, traffic-based network billing systems have the same requirement so that individual applications may be charged appropriately. In general, the same traffic statistics used for billing are required for capacity management.

Determine the level of detail of the information collected from the level required by the modelling techniques and tools used to process it. As a guide, accuracy (ie a difference between estimates and actuals) of within 10% in message sizes and volumes is normally quite acceptable, and useful results may be obtained with an accuracy of within 20-25% of actual values.

Thirdly

Obtain service level requirements for each application, to determine the target performance.

The application information gathered in the above three tasks is complementary to (and may overlap with) the workload catalogue produced within the host CDB.

Finally

Gather information on the equipment comprising and attached to the network. This must include:

* identification of all circuits with their transmission speeds, whether they are half or full duplex, where they originate and terminate (exchange areas) and their costs
* identification of all switching and multiplexing equipment, where individual items reside, their throughput and delay characteristics, their maximum capacities and their costs
* for multiplexed voice and data circuits, how the bandwidth is allocated on each such circuit
* detailed diagrams of the network topology and connectivity
* site information (this should positively identify all networked sites via addresses, telephone exchange area numbers and ideally, map references for wide area networks, and references to building plans showing cabling schemes for local area networks)
* identification of communications equipment at each site which should include references to equipment rack installation and cabling diagrams
* identification of user equipment at each site attached to the network. This should include how many there are of each type of terminal, controller and computer, how are they connected, which applications they use and what are their performance characteristics; specifically, delays induced and throughput capacity. In many cases, the delays and throughput capacities will have negligible significance, but this is not always the case and therefore checking is required.

When dealing with networks and associated equipment, it is useful to remember that a picture is worth a thousand words. Therefore, obtain or produce annotated diagrams wherever possible. All of this information should be in the Network Database, although the diagrams are probably held separately, with references to them held in the database itself. If the information is not available there, the Network Capacity Manager must gather it from the appropriate people and copy it to the custodian for entry into the Network Database.

Annex D. Workload management

D.1 Introduction

Managing the organization's workloads is crucial to effective capacity management. The Capacity Manager needs to know for each workload: the resources it consumes, whether the workload volumes will increase and how to forecast that growth, and its impact on IT resources. This annex addresses the most important aspects of this work.

Note: This module has set demarcation lines between tasks carried out under Resource and Workload Management categories. The demarcation lines may differ in each organization: in particular the production of a schedule of resources (Resource profiles DB) is often classed as a resource management task.

D.2 Understand and categorize workloads

Classify each workload into types of work; ie interactive, timesharing and batch work. Break down the total load into individual workloads wherever possible, where each element corresponds to a discrete business application. For example, Accounts Payable may be a major workload and it should be broken down into TP, timesharing and batch, as appropriate.

Try to limit the number of workloads to manageable proportions; eg a maximum of 20 to 25 workload types. Small workloads, eg those which consume less than 1% of the CPU, can be grouped together.

On a system that runs multiple applications it is necessary to have suitable naming standards (transaction id, user id, job name/account code) to identify the users of resources. Where such standards are not in place it may not be possible to identify usage by business. (If not in existence naming standards should be introduced as soon as possible, at least for new applications). It may therefore be necessary to work at gross levels; eg TP, timesharing, batch and system overheads.

The next step is to analyze and understand the trends of each workload, discovering when the peaks occur and why they happen. This investigation should encompass short, medium and long-term trends.

A short-term trend may be the normal daily pattern of work. Many online workloads develop a fairly stable profile with a morning start-up, morning peak, lunchtime trough, afternoon peak and close down, as shown in Figure D.1. Variations may occur. For example:

* organizations which have a flexitime system for employees may find that the peaks are smoothed slightly as more work is done during the early morning and late afternoon
* systems that deal with mail correspondence may have early morning peaks.

Figure D.1: Short-term utilization

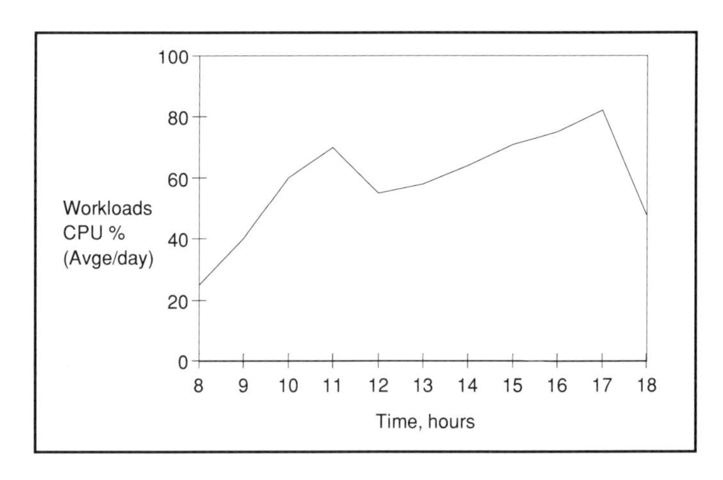

A medium trend may correspond to a monthly cycle. Many systems have monthly peaks, usually associated with accounting month-ends as shown in Figure D.2.

Figure D.2: Medium-term utilization

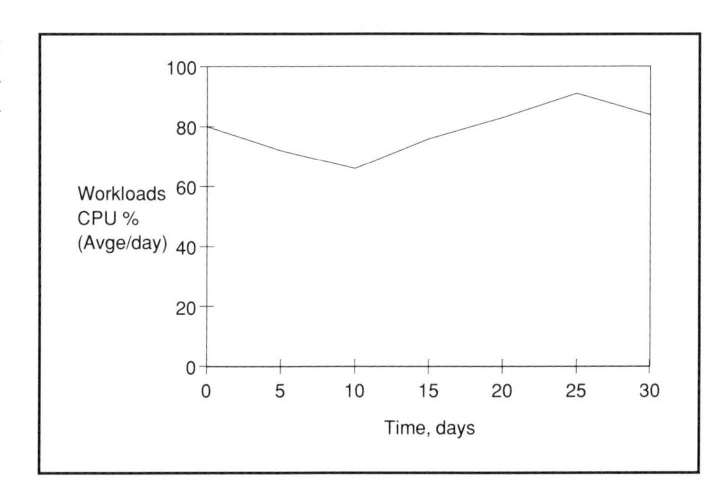

Figure D.3: Long-term utilization

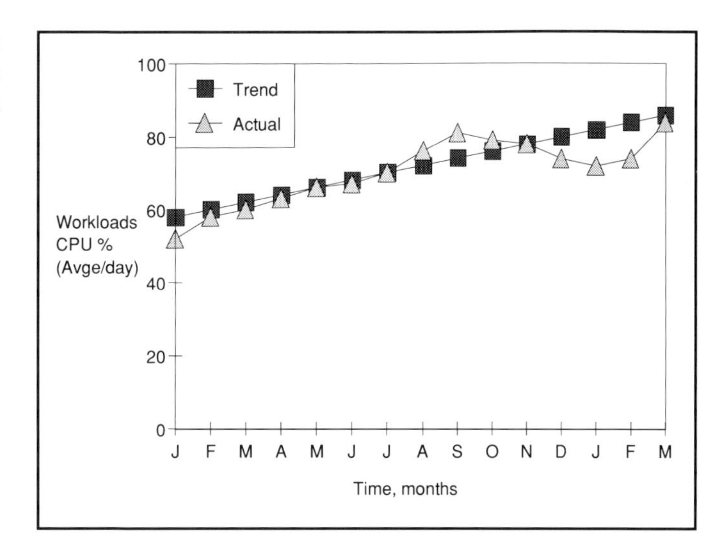

Many businesses have seasonal fluctuations, even if it is only end of fiscal year processing. See Figure D.3.

It is important to identify the 'time of planning concern' as soon as possible. That is, is it the intention to have sufficient capacity to meet the peak demand on the average day, the peak day that occurs every month, or the peak that only occurs for one week every year? This can only be determined when an understanding of the business has been obtained and the findings have been discussed with IT Management.

D.3 Resource profiles

Current and historical data should be available on transaction and job volumes plus the resources that they consume. However, as a precursor to forecasting it is recommended that a more detailed set of resource profiles are produced for each workload.

A resource profile describes the resource which an average unit of work consumes, ie:

* CPU
* disk/tape I/Os
* average input and output message sizes (TP only)
* memory occupancy.

WORKLOAD: xxx

Peak hour (1100-1200) resource profiles for week commencing 3/2/89

Transaction (work unit)	Frequency	Av. CPU (ms)	Av. No. of I/Os	Av. Input message length	Av. Output message length
MENU1	2473	82	1.3	8	206
MENU2	2735	27	0.8	5	107
ENQ1	1507	143	8.4	23	610
ENQ2	493	206	14.6	14	806
ENQ3	1120	172	10.8	10	425
UPDT1	745	253	18.6	162	107
UPDT2	1215	275	20.2	95	123

Figure D.4: Standard TP resource profiles

In general, for TP systems a work unit will usually be a message pair (computer transaction); for timesharing systems it can be expressed in message pairs or in terms of users; batch work units are jobs; office system or decision support work is usually represented in terms of users. An example profile for peak hour resource use is shown in Figure D.4.

Examples:

* the average enquiry transaction in the online personnel system uses 206 milliseconds of CPU and performs 14.6 physical I/Os; the average input message is 14 characters and the average output message is 806 characters

* a heavy timesharing user uses 2% of the CPU and performs 3 I/Os per second (similar profiles will be required for light and medium users)

* the monthly trial balance production job uses 1,650 seconds of CPU and performs 250,000 I/Os

* an average user of decision support uses 5% of the CPU and performs 4 I/Os per second.

Derive resource profiles from the detailed technical data which is kept in the CDB. It is recommended that software is written to automate the production of resource profiles since an up-to-date set should be produced prior to each forecasting exercise.

The capacity planner must be careful when calculating resource profiles to include all relevant data. For example, the TP measurements may only account for 60-70% of the total CPU which has been consumed by a transaction. The usual reason for this situation is that some synchronous system usage, both within the controlling TP software and the operating system, cannot be attributed to the transactions. I/O interrupt handling is one example of this phenomenon. The sum of all such synchronous overheads should be attributed to the transactions by 'prorating' them according to the level of CPU or I/O resources which were reported against the transactions by the TP statistics, ie spreading the overhead cost across each of the transactions. (Advice should be sought from the hardware manufacturer as to what the overheads correspond to, before deciding whether to calculate ratios on a CPU or I/O basis). Although the above example refers to a TP system, unallocated overheads must be taken into account in a similar manner for all other types of work.

D.4 Workload catalogue

The workload catalogue describes the current baseline of individual workloads.

When the individual workloads have been identified and their impact on the usage of hardware resources has been understood it is valuable to compile a catalogue which documents key facts about each existing and proposed workload. Note that this information can be incorporated into the service catalogue which is detailed in the Service Level Management module. Examples of items which can be held in the catalogue include:

* workload name and description
* job class
* dispatching and scheduling priorities
* times when the online service is available or times when batch jobs are run
* business volumes and frequencies
* frequencies (ie transaction or job volumes)
* special period-end processing requirements
* service level objectives

* resource profiles of the major transaction or job types
* disk space allocated
* any other information which may be considered useful.

Distribute the draft version of the catalogue widely within IT and ask for details of all discrepancies and any suggestions for the improvement of the catalogue. Incorporate agreed changes, publish the catalogue and update it when necessary.

D.5 Workload forecasting

Perform workload forecasting on a regular basis, eg quarterly. It should cover the planning horizon on a quarter-by-quarter basis.

In essence, forecasts are obtained by applying the results of all planned changes in demand to the existing use of the hardware resources. Therefore, the prerequisites are:

* an understanding of how a software change can affect hardware usage
* detailed understanding of the existing use of hardware resources, as discussed earlier in this section, and of the rate of change in usage
* an understanding of how workload changes can affect use of hardware or software
* details of all planned changes, both hardware and software
* anticipated volumes.

All of these items should be included in the catalogue.

D.6 Interviews

Obtain information relating to planned changes by carrying out a fact finding exercise. This is accomplished by talking to everyone who can usefully contribute to the production of a complete picture, including:

* Users
* IT management

* Service Level Manager
* Problem and Change Manager
* Applications Development Manager
* Network Manager
* Software Support Manager.

Whenever possible, face-to-face meetings should be held in preference to written communication. A personal relationship can be established and more detailed information can be elicited. In a meeting, do not use technical jargon. Try to elicit from them:

* projected business growth/decline. If there is a business plan in existence check that it is still valid; eg that the projected 15% annual growth has not been reduced to 10% in the light of experience. The Capacity Manager must be able to translate business growth/decline into computer transactions and jobs
* any changes in functionality. Changes can affect the amount of resource which a transaction/job consumes; eg if the amount of validation which is performed prior to an update transaction being accepted is to be altered, then this may lead to significant, additional processing, especially if extra database accesses are required. In addition, changes in functionality may affect transaction/job volumes. For example, if a new client enquiry service is being developed which will significantly assist the business, then this facility may dramatically increase the volume of transactions
* any changes in working patterns. Alterations to business practices or working hours, or even holidays, may have an impact on the demand. For example, the introduction of flexitime may reduce or move the daily peak loading
* details of new applications and planned implementation dates. In theory, this information should already be known. Check that implementation dates will be met and that customers are ready to use the new systems
* changes in staff profiles or branch numbers. Such changes may affect the demand

* changes in the terminal population. Such changes may affect transaction volumes, particularly if there is some form of latent demand. One method of forecasting for latent demand is to allow for one extra transaction per minute per terminal during peak processing periods. This figure can be altered according to local knowledge, eg a very busy system (data capture or application development) may entail one transaction per terminal every 30 or 45 seconds, a light system may involve one every 2 minutes.

Users may have difficulty in providing precise information on growth/decline, especially during the first forecasting exercise. In this situation, assist the user by asking for possible minimum and maximum values and validate their predictions against current trends, thus providing some basis for discussion and the subsequent derivation of an agreed mean figure.

Never try to pin the user to a single, rigid figure; eg growth will be 20% per annum. Attempt to agree upper and lower bounds; eg the mean is likely to be 20% but it could be as little as 10%, or as much as 30%. It is preferable to perform some sensitivity analysis by producing three sets of forecasts, viz optimistic (lower bound), likely (median) and pessimistic (upper bound). This will give some degree of confidence in the results.

Discussions with IT Management should centre on any changes which may not yet be common knowledge. For example, a pilot office automation or decision support system might be under consideration. Perhaps even new DBMS software; maximum forewarning of all such changes is required.

The Application Development Manager can provide information on the status of all development work and any changes in their own working patterns; eg the use of CASE tools, application generators, 4GLs. Size the impact of any changes. 4GLs in particular can be very resource intensive. It is recommended that resource profiles are obtained for light, medium and heavy users. Preferably obtain this information from other users of the same products, or failing that from in-house benchmarks or from the vendor.

The Network Manager can detail any changes to the organization's telecommunications infrastructure.

The Software Support Manager can provide details of any planned changes to the operating software. Obtain details of any increased overheads from existing users of the same products, from in-house benchmarks or from the vendor.

The Change Manager coordinates planned hardware or software changes which may affect the forecasts.

The Service Level Manager can provide particulars of the transaction/volumes which are to be supported by each workload.

It may appear from the above that similar questions are being asked of different individuals. This is quite deliberate since it will highlight any inconsistencies which are present, due either to misunderstanding, lack of communication or lack of factual information.

D.7 Hardware forecasts

Calculate CPU and I/O resource forecasts (these being the most obvious to begin with) for each workload during the time of planning concern eg the peak hour - using the formula:

$$F_t = \sum_{i=1}^{n} (U_i \times R_i)$$

where:

n is the number of resource profiles

F_t is the total number of forecasts

i is the individual forecast, predicted unit of demand or resource profile.

U is the predicted units of demand; eg the number of message pairs, the number of users, or the number of jobs

R is the resource profile; ie the amount of CPU and I/O resources which are consumed by one unit.

The Capacity Manager should use the accumulated knowledge of the existing system to transform estimated business growth/decline into units of demand. Be aware that not all demand may be directly related to business growth/decline. For example, a large percentage of the enquiries on a TP system may be related to the size of the terminal population. The Capacity Manager should attempt to isolate such items and treat them separately.

Conversely, an increase in the size of the terminal population may, or may not, be solely related to business growth. As terminals proliferate, more use is made of the enquiries services; it then often appears that growth in terminal population is directly proportional to the number of enquiry transactions!

For workloads where the unit of demand is one customer, the Capacity Manager should attempt to categorize customers as light, medium and heavy users, if there are discrete resource profiles for each level of usage.

When the functionality of an application is changed, the capacity planner needs to amend the existing resource profile. If the amended program code already exists then obtain the new profiles by running a benchmark and monitoring the results. If the program code does not yet exist then the Capacity Manager has to estimate the new resource profile. Guidance on how to do this is given in Annex F, Application Sizing. If application sizing has not yet been tackled, increase the resource profile in direct proportion to the increase in the amount of logical database accessing. If the logical accesses are unknown, increase the profile by a set percentage, based on discussion with the application developers.

Appropriate applications must also be included in the forecasts. Guidance is given on this subject in Annex E. If application sizing has not yet been implemented, use any existing sizing techniques or the "rule of thumb" techniques which are also described in Annexes I and J.

Note that the Capacity Manager must account for all system overheads such as system tasks, spooling, monitors, communications software and so on. These overheads vary from machine to machine and depend on the operating software and the products which are installed. Monitor the system to obtain the actual overhead. The overhead typically varies in relation to the overall machine load. As a rule of thumb, large mainframes may experience overheads of 15-30%. Small to medium-sized machines may have an overhead of 10%.

Obtain disk space requirements forecasts for all applications from the database administrator. Obtain system requirements for extra space, eg larger spool, more page files or new products from the Systems Support Manager and any other relevant parties. Note that some organizations may already have a person who is responsible for storage management. That person should be able to provide all disk space forecasts.

Produce forecasts then for:

* CPU
* disks
* tapes
* print
* networks
* memory (storage)
* minor peripherals.

Ensure that any disaster or contingency plan is updated as appropriate.

D.8 Reports

From the forecasting exercise produce a plan with appropriate graphs. A suggested framework for the report is:

* management summary
* current hardware needs to support the business
* scope of the forecasts (including any noticeable omissions)
* future hardware needs
* all major assumptions; eg the office automation system will be implemented in the 1st Quarter (Q1) 1992; business growth is estimated at 20%
* graphs at the business level with more detailed information; eg at application level, in tabular form
* a statement on the degree of confidence which can be placed on the results, detailing the possible effects on those results if any of the major assumptions prove to be incorrect
* conclusions, options and recommendations.

Some ideas about the sort of information which can be presented graphically are in Annex L.

Annex E. Modelling

E.1 Modelling

Modelling has been described in this module as one of the major elements of capacity management. It can be used to beneficial effect in the majority of capacity management tasks:

* performance management and impact of tuning proposals
* workload forecasting
* application sizing
* service level management
* cost management
* production of the capacity plan
* resource management.

This annex is included to introduce the need for modelling tools and how they are used. Figure E.1, overleaf, outlines the role of modelling.

The techniques available for capacity planning range from, at one extreme, estimation (ie guesswork based on experience), to at the other extreme, pilot studies and benchmarking the prototype. The former is cheap and is a reasonable approach for day-to-day small decisions, whereas the latter is expensive but may be considered prudent when implementing a very large new project.

Between these two extremes are three techniques which are much less risky than estimation and much cheaper than prototyping. These are, in ascending order of cost and accuracy:

* trend analysis (cheapest)
* analytic modelling
* simulation (most accurate).

Trend analysis will typically only provide utilizations, it will not produce response times and it is therefore inappropriate where service level agreements are employed; it is of no value in forecasting the effects of workload changes. Analytic modelling and simulation each has its own merits and its own suitability to particular tasks, as discussed in this section.

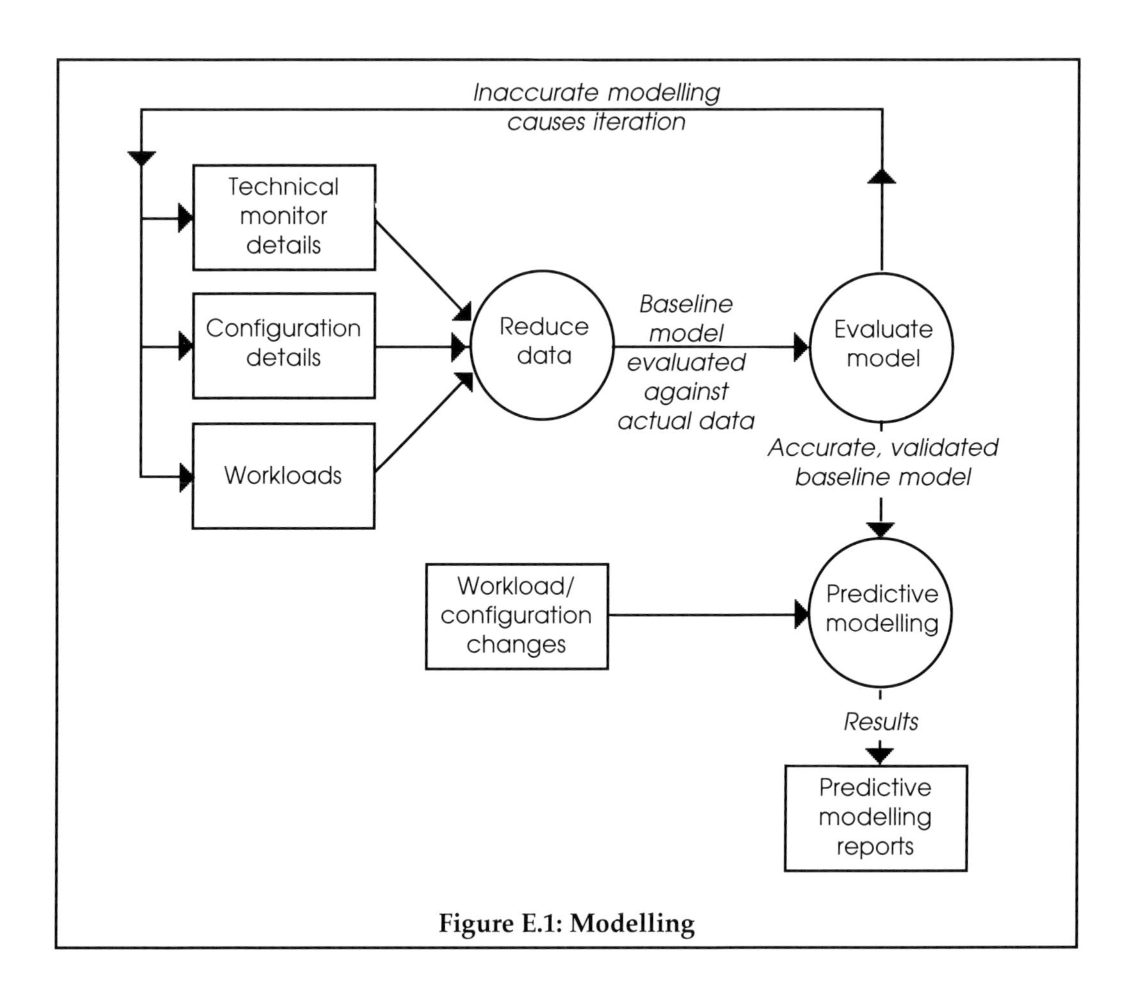

Figure E.1: Modelling

E.2 Mainframe (host) modelling

The ability to predict the behaviour of computer systems under a given volume and variety of work is a fundamental requirement for capacity management. The calculation of utilizations for individual hardware components is a relatively straightforward task if it is known how frequently service is required from each device; eg the number of I/Os to a disk per hour, and what the average service time is for each request; eg 25 milliseconds for an I/O. A spreadsheet could be used for this purpose.

However, utilizations are only part of the answer. Since IT Services is trying to provide a quality service to its users, it is imperative that capacity management is able to predict online response times and batch turnaround times. This involves the use of queueing theory. Although the Capacity

Manager could develop a system to calculate queueing times, path delays and thus response times, it is a complex subject which should be avoided except by mathematicians who have the time and knowledge to develop such a system.

Fortunately, there are modelling products available which will perform the tasks and produce utilizations, queueing times, path delays, response times etc. There are two types of tools - simulation and analytical modelling.

Simulation involves modelling of discrete events; eg transactions, against a given hardware configuration, and is especially accurate in sizing new applications. The products typically contain the performance characteristics of individual hardware and software components. Simulation gives very accurate results. Unfortunately, it can be very time consuming to set up the input to the model. Simulation will be invaluable for very large systems where the cost (tens of £m) and associated performance implications assume great importance.

Analytical models are representations of the behaviour of computer systems using mathematical techniques. They are based on multi-class network queueing theory. The breakthrough for this branch of mathematics came in the early seventies - see figure E.2.

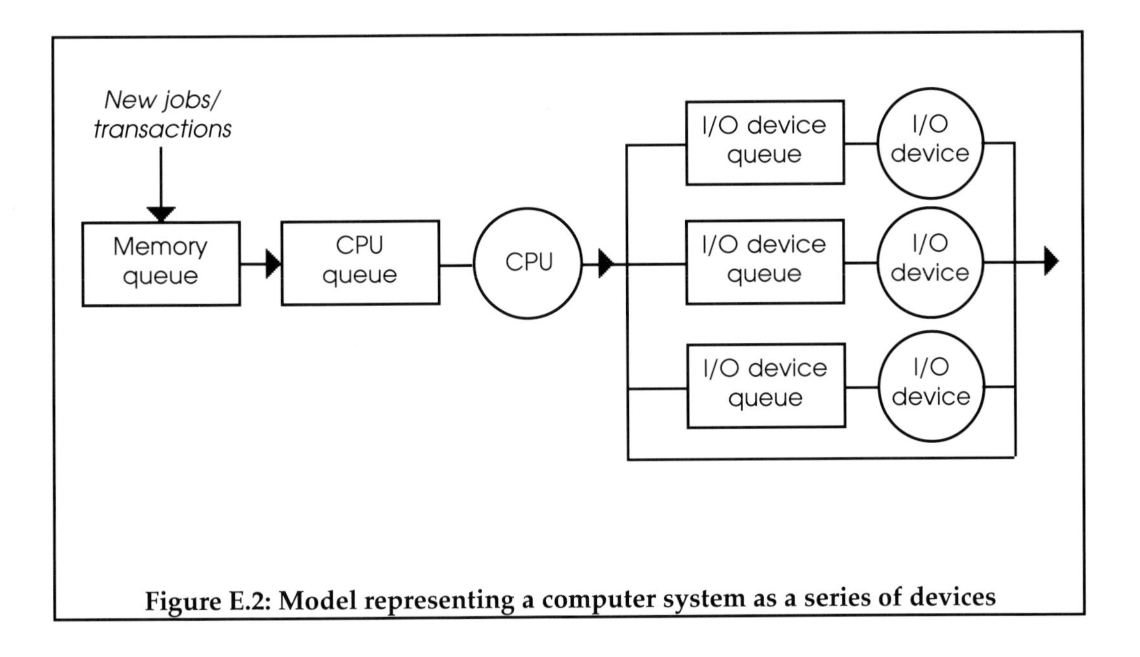

Figure E.2: Model representing a computer system as a series of devices

Network queueing theory is suitable for capacity management purposes because it:

* examines all of the theoretical queues and the likelihood of resource contention
* takes into account overlapping of resource usage (which arises from multiprogramming)
* uses a small, finite number, ie the actual number of customers, in the queueing system
* uses the arrival pattern at a server as determined by the overall system characteristics
* takes into account the effect of dispatching priorities
* has the ability to specify different classes of concurrent workloads with different characteristics.

The analytical modelling technique demands less effort from the capacity planner, but it typically gives less accurate results than simulation. However, the results are usually satisfactory for the purposes of capacity planning. Seek a level of accuracy which is within 5% for all utilizations, and within 15-20% for response times and batch turnaround times. It is important to calibrate the model so that these target percentages can be achieved.

E.3 Baseline models

The first stage in the modelling process is to create a model of the current system, where one exists, during the period of planning concern; eg the peak hour. The objective is to ensure that this model, which is usually termed the baseline model, accurately reflects the performance which is actually achieved. When an accurate baseline model has been created predictive modelling can begin.

The information which is required for the baseline model is typically derived from the system monitor (time driven) data and from accounting data (event driven). Software interfaces are available with some modelling products for given hardware/software environments to automate the reduction of the data into a form which can be put directly into the model. Manual reduction can be a time-consuming exercise (2-3 days depending on the system), especially on the first occasion that it is attempted. This time-consuming task initially ensures that the workload components, identified collectively represent the entire loading of the system. The task also includes identification for each workload of:

* CPU/OCP usage
* disc I/Os
* batch stream concurrencies
* TP message pair rates
* system overheads (interrupt handling costs)
* system tasks.

It is highly recommended that the Capacity Manager should use the manual reduction method at least once, even if a software interface is available, as it teaches the Capacity Manager a great deal about the behaviour of the computer system, of which they might otherwise be unaware; eg the existence of spikes in performance.

The input of the hardware configuration details into the model is a straightforward process with the possible exception that some monitors do not allow the average service time of I/O devices to be derived.

In addition, it may be necessary to obtain details of the connectivity of the I/O subsystem from a configuration diagram.

The total volume of work which is running on the hardware is split up into discrete workloads. The manner in which the workloads are derived is dictated by what planning questions need to be answered; eg a workload may be synonymous with a type of work (interactive, batch, timesharing), a business or an individual application.

For individual applications factors include:

* the level of detail which is provided by the monitors
* a restriction in the software pertaining to the number of workloads which can be defined in a single model.

Individual workloads can typically be modelled in one of three ways:

* a workload characterized by the random arrival of jobs or transactions, each being processed as it arrives (subject to a predefined maximum concurrency) as shown in figure E.3. This method can be used for all types of work, eg online, batch and system tasks

Figure E.3: Representation of a transaction processing workload

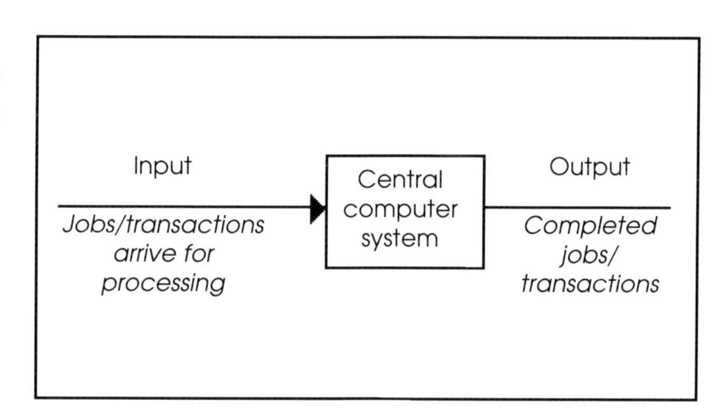

* the throughput is dictated by the number of concurrently active terminals and the average think/ type time (and, of course, the activity of all the other workloads). The term 'think/type time' is defined as the time taken from when a reply for a terminal leaves the host, to the arrival at the host of the next input message from that terminal. See figure E.4. This model is suitable for online systems only (usually timesharing work)

Figure E.4: Representation of a terminal driven workload

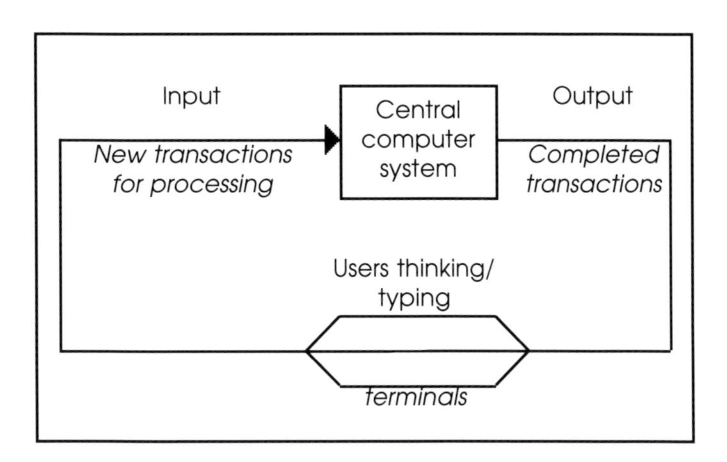

* the throughput is dictated by the number of concurrent batch streams which always have a backlog of work (and, of course, the activity of all the other workloads), as shown in figure E.5. This model is suitable only for batch work which meets the backlog criterion.

Figure E.5: Representation of a backlog workload

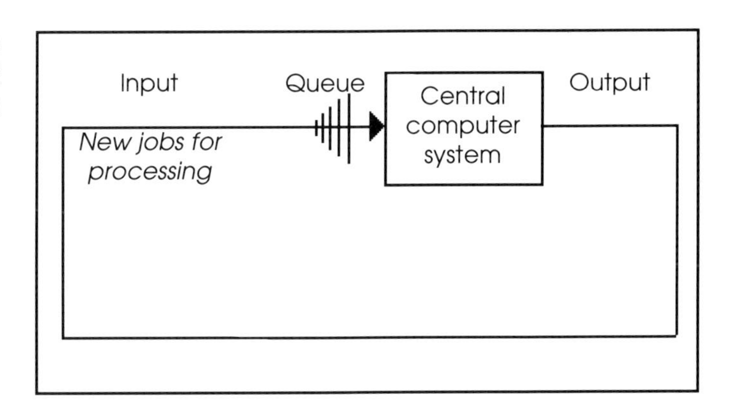

Finally, the model will contain the resource profiles for each workload. This is the amount of CPU and the number of I/Os by device which have been consumed by a single work unit (eg one transaction or job). Some products also allow the average memory occupancy of each workload to be specified. It is the production of these resource profiles which consumes 95+% of the total time taken to construct a model manually.

Many monitors do not provide the data which is necessary to obtain the I/Os which are performed for each workload by device. In that case, it will be necessary for the Capacity Manager to use his/her knowledge of where files are situated to decide how a workload's I/Os should be distributed. Note that the total I/O for a device across all workloads must equal the figure which is reported against that device by the system monitor.

When the complete model has been constructed it is run (the usual term is evaluated). The results are then validated against the actual monitored figures. As stated above, utilizations should be within 5% and response times within 15-20% of the actual figures. Any inaccuracies should be investigated and corrected.

Some of the common reasons for inaccuracies include:

* keying errors while inputting the model
* arithmetic errors which occurred during manual model construction
* additional delays which have not been accounted for such as software locks and operator delays; eg waiting for a tape mount. (Some products allow fixed delays to be incorporated into the model in the form of a hardware server which has no queueing, but merely imposes a specified delay).

The Capacity Manager should ensure that utilizations are within 5%, before progressing to predictive modelling. However, if response times of the desired accuracy cannot be obtained, and if, after investigation, there appears to be no reason for that discrepancy, then the Capacity Manager may elect to commence predictive modelling, on the proviso that the discrepancy is taken into account when assessing the results of any predictive model.

If this is the case consider the possibilities that:

* architecture was not correctly specified
* applications are behaving in a different manner to predictions.

E.4 Predictive modelling

When the baseline model has been validated, ask planning (what if) questions which reflect changes to the hardware and/or the volume/variety of workloads. The majority of modelling tools which are available allow the user to change any of the basic elements of a model; eg:

* CPU
* disk characteristics including speed
* add/remove devices, controllers and channels
* alter the I/O connectivity
* change the volume of transactions for a given workload
* alter the CPU priority or multi programming level (mpl) of a workload
* alter the resource profile of a workload
* alter the terminal concurrency level or think-type time
* alter the number of batch streams
* add/remove workloads.

The Capacity Manager assesses the results of each predictive model to ensure that service levels can be maintained and that no major bottlenecks appear. If service levels are exceeded then appropriate corrective action has to be taken, typically by reducing the demand or by upgrading the hardware.

E.5 Network modelling

The approach should be to take two passes at data collection. First collect what seems appropriate for an existing system, build a model with it and compare the results it produces with the real system. By making changes to the collected data, the sensitivity to change becomes quickly apparent and also the areas where better or more data is needed. The second pass is to gather revised data from these areas and rebuild the model. Again, a difference of 10% between the final model results and the real system is quite acceptable.

For each site, build a model of the site traffic flowing on the links between associated computer locations. This should take into account every circuit and piece of equipment likely to cause a delay in the path of the traffic. Although this can be done by hand, this is not recommended since it is very time consuming and error prone because of the large amount of arithmetic involved. For those interested in the theory or in actually carrying out manual calculations, further information on this subject can be found in the standard reference work 'Systems Analysis for Data Transmission' by James Martin, published by Prentice-Hall. A better approach is to use a computer-based modelling tool, of which there are several available on the market. These tools fall into two groups, simulation and queueing theory. Each method has its advantages and disadvantages. Choose the appropriate one for the task in hand.

Simulation

Simulation examines the flow of individual messages through a network. It is particularly accurate and appropriate for examining transient conditions and problems. However, it requires a large volume of input data, accurately described, if all the messages flowing in a given time period are to form part of the simulation. As a technique it also requires large amounts of computer time to produce individual results. Runs then have to be repeated, varying the data each time, to obtain results relating to average conditions.

Analytic modelling

Analytic modelling considers aggregated traffic, rather than individual messages, and treats it in a statistical manner. Thus it is inherently less accurate than simulation. On the other hand, it requires much less data than simulation to produce meaningful and realistic results. These results relate to steady state situations, which may vary from the peak few minutes to the monthly average depending upon the analysis required. Compared with simulation, analytic modelling produces much quicker results although they are less accurate. However, the accuracy of the technique is proportional to that of the input data and thus expect the results of a good model to be within 10% of the measured figures. To construct a good model build a prototype of a known system for which data is available from some months ago; then, vary the model conditions in line with what happened as time passed up to the present day; finally compare the results with today's situation, and the discrepancies show the inherent error of the model. These discrepancies may then be accepted and the model maintained or alternatively, calibration variables may be altered within the model until its behaviour corresponds to the real world.

As to the choice of technique, high level traffic planning of the E-mail and X.400 systems is likely to benefit from simulation. On the other hand, transaction processing and file transfer traffic through a wide area network may be modelled much more cost-effectively using queueing theory. Section 7 gives details of currently available tools of each type.

LAN

Local area networks are a special case. Under normal circumstances, the terminal population of a local area network is very small in relation to the available bandwidth. The terminal population has to be numbered in hundreds on a 10Mbps (Megabyte per second) ISO 8802/3 ('Ethernet'-type) LAN before the LAN itself imposes traffic bottlenecks. The causes of impaired response times and throughput are file servers, bridges and gateways. These are, in queueing theory terms, single-server queues and may be treated as such. In situations of complex traffic where transient effects are important, simulation is more useful than analytic modelling - but the effort expended may not be worthwhile in cost effectiveness cost or benefit terms.

Once a model has been built and calibrated, the resultant capacity it reveals for each user service may be examined and compared with the actual traffic flowing, as determined from performance monitoring statistics. This shows how much (if any) capacity is left.

Use of graphs

There are two significant graphs to use when analyzing performance for network capacity management purposes. See figures E.6 and E.7.

The first is the variation of response time with line utilization. An example is shown in figure E.6. This may be drawn from collected performance data, but more often the Network Capacity Manager will produce it using the model and then check it for accuracy against real data. Its function is to show where the performance begins to deteriorate rapidly as a result of congestion. Aim to keep line utilization below the 'knee' in the curve so as to maintain performance levels which satisfy service level agreements.

Figure E.6: Response time vs line utilization

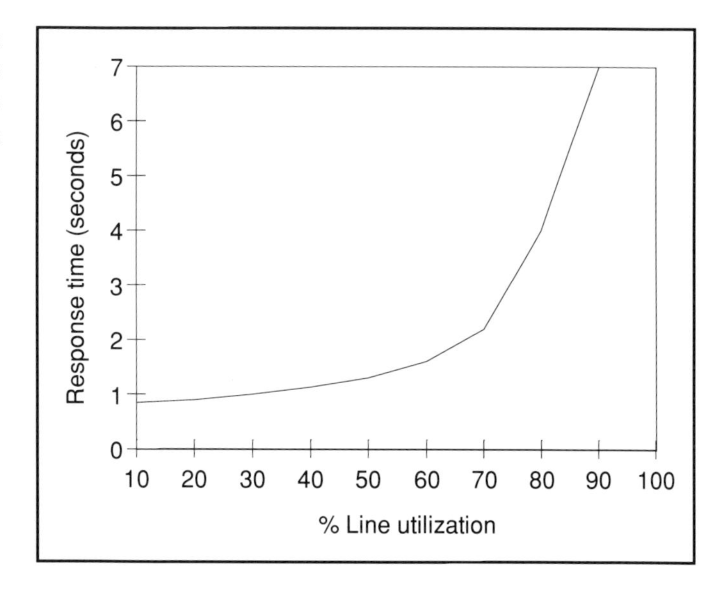

Figure E.7: Traffic volume vs response time

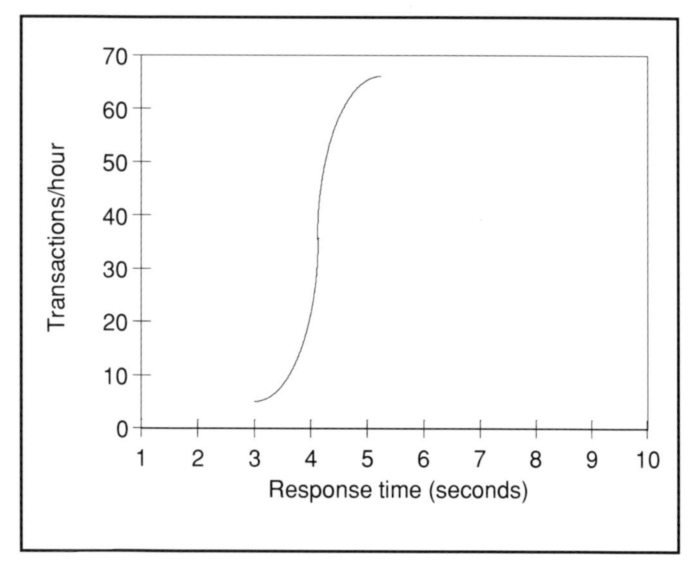

How close to the 'knee' depends on the confidence in, ie the accuracy of, the data used by the model. As utilization creeps nearer this point on the live network, so the actual performance needs more careful monitoring. In practice this curve frequently shows the 'knee' at about 70% utilization. This is the reason for the 'rule of thumb' frequently used by network designers of keeping line utilization below this figure.

The second graph, shown in figure E.7, shows the variation of response time with traffic. This is a measure of response time consistency and the use of this information is important in achieving cost-effective network performance. The steeper the curve, the more consistent the response time, and a good consistent response time is the target.

Performance levels are primarily concerned with what users need, not what they necessarily ask for. Needs are established by human behaviour patterns, thus a consistent, predictable response is always more important than the absolute value of a response time, as has already been mentioned in the section on tuning. Therefore the aim of the Network Capacity Manager should be to plan for and maintain consistent response times. Once these have been achieved, the task is to reduce these response times without losing the consistency. In general, reducing the response times in this manner costs money, through the use of greater transmission capacity. It is the Network Capacity Manager's duty to calculate the options available in terms of performance improvements and costs incurred, so that the Service Level Manager has the necessary information to negotiate SLAs with users.

Monitoring topology

A major difference between computer capacity management and wide area network capacity management lies in the fact that the bulk of the network investment is in revenue items, specifically in circuit rentals. The Network Capacity Manager therefore has the opportunity to monitor existing traffic levels and to see whether the topology of the network still fits the traffic requirements. If not, then the effects of topology changes on performance and costs should be examined. This is a significant task done manually, but is relatively straightforward with network design and costing tools now commercially available. Again, details of tools are given in section 7. The potential savings here are significant and should not be ignored. However, this task is not necessary if a policy decision has been made to carry all wide-area network traffic via a third-party network. Even so, it is a worthwhile exercise to carry out to quantify the benefits (or otherwise) of using a third-party network. In the case of a user committed to a commercial Value Added Network Service (VANS), the Network Capacity Manager's task is to compare one VANS offering against another, given the known and planned traffic, to determine the best available cost/ performance ratio to meet the organization's needs.

Another difference between host and network capacity planning is that even though there may be no change in average computer utilization, there may be a complete change in network utilization as a group of users in one geographic area finishes work and a group in another area starts. Knowledge of these traffic pattern changes is crucial to effective provision of network capacity.

The Network Manager should ensure that regular cost reviews are undertaken and reports produced. These reviews comprise a reappraisal of all circuit usage to determine where circuits have become redundant and where traffic rerouteing can be made to save circuits. Care must be taken not to damage resilience and future project plans through over-zealous pruning. The report mentioned above is a critical element in maintaining a cost-effective network. It should be produced at time intervals in line with the receipt of PTO bills, normally quarterly.

Contingency

A further task for the Network Capacity Manager is to establish the amount of contingency required. This takes two forms; backup lines in the event of line or packet switch failure, for example and backup network equipment and lines to connect to a standby computer centre. In each case, establish the cost and performance implications so that backup service levels can be defined. Again, this is an area where skilful use of modelling and costing tools can save significant amounts of investment on existing and planned backup arrangements.

Last, but by no means least, the information in the models is used for forward planning by the Network Capacity Manager to predict:

* the effect of site movements on cost and performance
* the effect of growth in applications traffic on network capacity, in order to predict the likely life of the current investment
* the changes required to the network to accommodate new applications without impairing current application service levels.

All of the above are applications of the techniques already described for current modelling. In this way, the best available current information is used to remove the guesswork from network planning.

Annex F. Application sizing

F.1 Application sizing

Figure F.1 is a simplified representation of application sizing. Sizing of new applications, or major changes to existing applications, is a very important aspect of capacity management. Unfortunately, this subject is the least well understood. The primary objective of sizing is to estimate the hardware resources which are needed to support the proposed application and provide the required service levels. Sizing is particularly beneficial in the early stages of a project when any cost implications must be taken into account in justifying the proposed application to senior management.

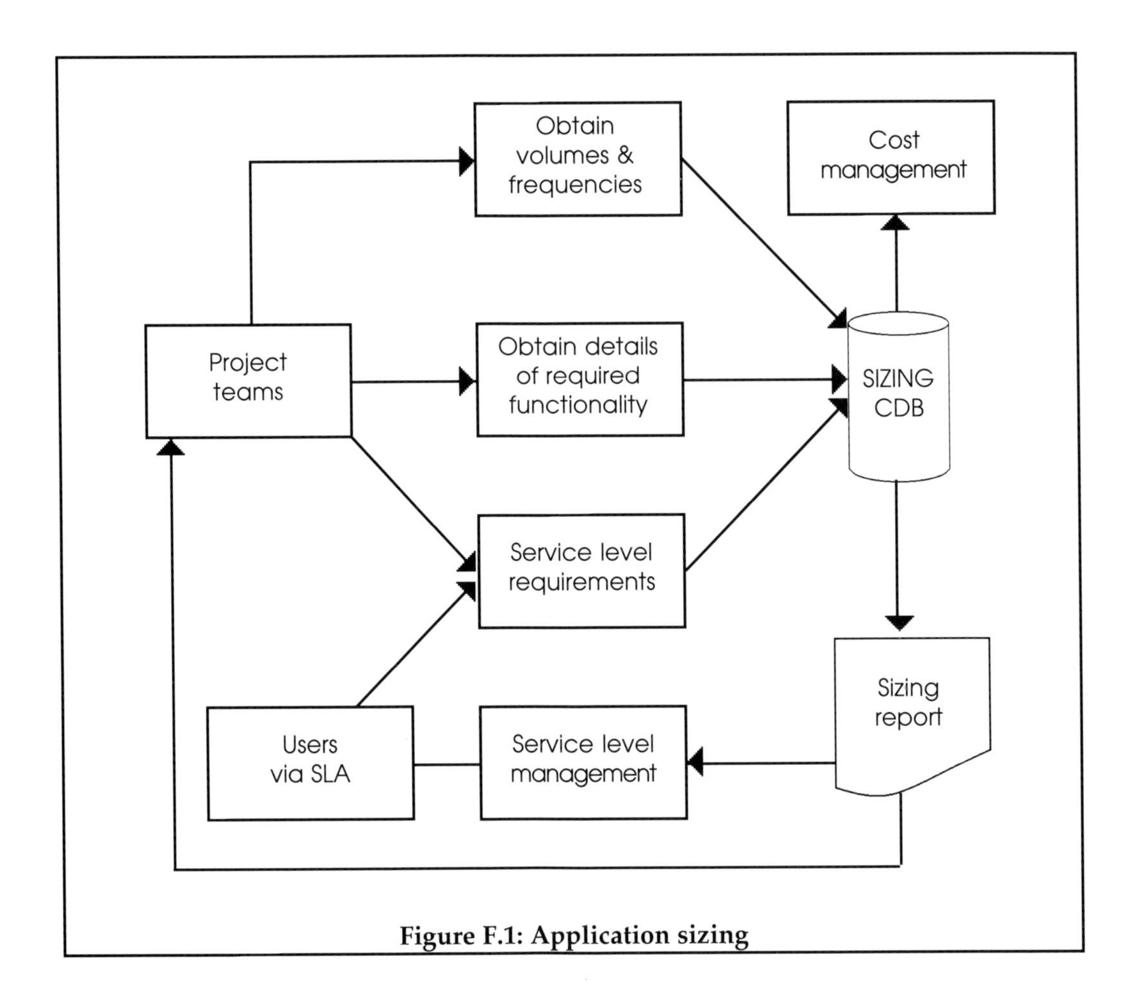

Figure F.1: Application sizing

F.2 Preparation

Preparation for the introduction of application sizing should include:

* an awareness campaign for application developers
* a review of, and amendments to, the current design standards
* a review of sizing tools.

F.3 Awareness campaign

It is important that the Capacity Manager wins the support and confidence of the application developers. An awareness campaign, similar to the one that was recommended in 3.1.6.11, in the form of formal presentations with written backup material, will help the Capacity Manager to break down any barriers. The major topics should include:

* why capacity management is necessary
* what is capacity management
* the need to size applications at all stages of the development lifecycle
* the benefits to the application developers in terms of feedback on the proposed design; viz estimated service levels, details of those elements of the application which are likely to suffer poor performance and any cost implications.

F.4 Review standards

Application sizing must be an integral part of the development lifecycle, if it is to be effective. It should not be regarded as an additional encumbrance which is outside the scope and responsibility of the project team (often the normal state of affairs). Overcome this problem by making the project manager responsible for the delivery of an application which not only contains the desired functionality and ease of use, but which can also meet the agreed service levels. Therefore, it is recommended that the sizing activity is scheduled into every design phase of the lifecycle and that the results of the sizing form part of the deliverable from each phase (see 3.1.6 and Capacity management and design methodologies, below).

The Capacity Manager must review the current development standards to discover how application sizing is dealt with during the lifecycle and what relevant data items are available. Carry out this review with the knowledge and co-operation of application development staff.

Capacity management and design methodologies

Design methodologies and standards have not addressed the needs of capacity management satisfactorily in the past. Minor references such as 'Perform Sizing' are commonly found. This situation is beginning to change. The subject guide describing SSADM V4 and Capacity Planning begins to address this omission.

Information systems have been specified largely on the basis of their functionality. Less emphasis has been placed on the required levels of functionality that the application should deliver in order to satisfy the needs of the business. This further dimension of functionality must be described in terms of service levels, detailed in the Service Level Management module. Amongst the criteria used to evaluate the results of capacity modelling insofar as new applications are concerned are response times, throughput, arrival rates and so on.

What the developer can do

During systems analysis and design, the levels of functionality can be described in terms of service level objectives. As these objectives become established during the development of the application they are formalized as Service Level Requirements which in turn, as part of the process of implementation and acceptance, are incorporated in a Service Level Agreement.

The accuracy of any modelling approach is dependent upon the accuracy of the data used to build the models. It is possible to employ capacity planning techniques for evaluating new applications and to obtain results that will be acceptable. Exact precision is unlikely, but the degree of accuracy will represent a marked improvement on current estimating techniques. Capacity planning techniques enable the applications developers to work towards the following objectives:

* to enable the service level objectives for the proposed application to be tested in terms of achievability, reasonableness and cost effectiveness. This is a powerful way of looking at the contribution made by a proposed information system towards satisfying business objectives

* to assess the impact of the new application on the existing infrastructure and relevant Service Level Agreements

* to estimate the hardware requirements of the new application (sizing).

What the Capacity Manager can do

Some metrics, particularly data volumes and transaction frequencies, are usually found in system specifications. However, it is not unusual to find that the specification is not being adhered to; ie the metrics are omitted. The Capacity Manager should check for adherence to the specification and point out any non-conformance.

Sometimes, required data items, eg access paths, may be produced as a by-product of the development, but they may not form part of the published output from any of the phases. In this instance the Capacity Manager should seek to include such items.

The data items required by the Capacity Manager for each business function are described below (however, note that many of the items are unlikely to be available before the logical design stage. Methods of sizing applications during the earlier stages are discussed later in this section):

* business function identity

* business function description

* type of processing (online or batch)

* enquiry or update

* frequency - average day/hour, peak day/hour, or any particular idiosyncracies; eg 40% of the daily frequency occurs in a two-hour window

* average number of computer transactions per invocation of the business function (online only)

* average input/output message sizes (online only)

* average number of logical database (or row) accesses per business invocation

* average number of physical database accesses per business invocation

* terminal requirements (quantity, type, geographic location)

* requirements for additional facilities; eg local processing (stand-alone PC, LAN based processing, access to facilities on other hosts).

From the review of the specification produce a written report which:

* summarizes the suitability of the current standards for application sizing
* highlights any obvious examples of wholesale non-conformance to the existing standards
* defines all data items which should be added to the standards in order that applications can be sized
* recommends when sizing exercises should be performed; ie at each stage of the development, from feasibility study through to physical design, as an integral part of those phases
* recommends the procedures for the monitoring of program code, when it is available, in order that modelling tools can be used to take the resultant resource profiles along with the estimated production volumes to obtain expected hardware utilizations and levels of service
* recommends stress testing of the completed application, where this is appropriate
* defines the deliverable from a sizing exercise.

Present the report informally to the Application Development Manager, the Service Level Manager and nominated members of the project team.

F.5 Review sizing tools

Finally, review the suitability of tools to assist the sizing process. Annex B and section 7 provide details of suggested criteria which can be used to evaluate application sizing tools. The majority of the existing tools are most effective when a detailed design of the application is available. However, the Capacity Manager needs to size the application during the earlier stages when the relevant information is scarce. The tools can be employed in this situation, with assumptions from the Capacity Manager, but they are not ideal.

Consider the compilation of relevant sizing facts and figures which can be employed either to supplement a sizing tool, or indeed possibly obviate the need for a tool.

These facts and figures may be obtained from vendors (not usual), other users of similar operating software or from detailed investigation of the organization's existing hardware/software platform. Examples are as follows:

* resource costs to resolve a soft page fault
* resource costs to resolve a hard page fault
* underlying resource cost overhead for an online transaction (excluding application specific items)
* resource costs of journalling
* resource costs of logging
* resource costs per logical database access
* resource costs per physical database access
* resource costs per terminal input/output
* resource costs per transaction for communication software
* estimated resource costs for simple, medium, complex and very complex transactions on a specified software platform, where the meaning of these adjectives is defined; eg a simple transaction performs 5 or less I/Os, medium is 6-15 I/Os, complex is 16-30 I/Os and very complex is greater than 30
* resource costs for each class of user, ie heavy, medium or light, of unstructured systems, eg application development or decision support
* asynchronous system tasks - typically represented as a percentage to be added to the total CPU utilization; eg if the system overhead is estimated to be 10% over a total CPU utilization of all non-system elements of 60% then the actual system overhead will be 6%.

Note that all resource cost figures should include any synchronous overheads. (See 4.1.4).

It is acknowledged that the compilation of the above items can be a long and arduous exercise if all the items have to be derived by personal investigation. However, the information will be most valuable.

F.6 Mainframe sizing

This sub-section describes various methods of sizing applications at different stages of development.

F.6.1 Crude sizing of bespoke applications

During the early stages of the development lifecycle, eg feasibility study and even functional specification, sizing information will perforce be scarce.

The Capacity Manager should obtain missing information through discussion with members of the project team. Persuade them to take a view on the proposed application if they seem reticent, after all, they must have better ideas than the Capacity Manager about the functionality of the application.

F.6.2 CPU and I/O sizing

The Capacity Manager should endeavour to assess the size and scope of the application; this will enable the Capacity Manager to gauge the overall impact.

For example, if the transaction volume is very low and the application will not be complex then it may be judged that its impact will be slight; eg 1% or less CPU utilization. This may be sufficient during the early stages.

However, if the application is considered to have a potentially larger impact on the existing system, it is necessary to try another approach.

Simplistically, the estimated CPU and I/O resources are calculated by multiplying the frequency of transactions or jobs by the average resource cost per invocation.

Derive transaction frequencies, if not known, from the terminal population. For example, estimate the frequency of transactions during the peak period by assuming one transaction from each terminal every:

* 30 seconds if it is likely to be a very busy system
* 60 seconds as the default
* 120 seconds for a low volume system.

One simple technique for the estimation of resource profiles is to relate the proposed application to an existing one; eg it will be similar to the personnel system. This method is only valid where both applications use the same software platform; eg the same TP Monitor and DBMS.

A better solution is to determine the complexity of the application; eg simple, medium, complex or very complex where the definition of each of these vague terms has been defined in terms of perhaps number of I/Os in the application (see also below, the example of crude sizing). Each level corresponds to specified resource costs on the target hardware and software platform. Note that four levels of complexity is merely an arbitrary range. Use more or less levels, as appropriate.

An entire application can be categorized as being medium. Alternatively, it can be classified as 40% simple, 40% medium and 20% complex.

Example of crude sizing

The following information is available:

* no transaction frequencies are available
* the application will support 200 terminals
* it is estimated by the project team that the application can be classified as 30% simple, 50% medium and 20% complex
* it has been decided, based on observation of other applications that:
    - a simple transaction will consume 50 milliseconds (ms) of CPU and perform 5 I/Os
    - a medium transaction will consume 100 ms of CPU and perform 10 I/Os
    - a complex transaction will consume 200 ms of CPU and perform 20 I/Os
* asynchronous system overheads are calculated to be 10% for the CPU, and 2.5% for I/O.

The manual calculations are as follows:

The peak hour transaction frequency is calculated as:

200 x 60 = 12000 transactions.

CPU resource costs are:

CPU=
[(12000 x 0.3) x 50ms] +
[(12000 x 0.5) x 100ms] +
[(12000 x 0.2) x 200ms]
= 1260 seconds.

Total I/O is:

I/O= [(12000 x 0.3) x 5] +
[(12000 x 0.5) x 10] +
[(12000 x 0.2) x 20]
= 126,000.

System overheads:

CPU= 126 seconds

I/O= 3150.

If response times are required then it is suggested that a modelling tool is used. The individual (or aggregate) items can be incorporated into a model of the existing system. The resultant model will produce hardware utilizations and service levels, not only for the new application, but also for the existing workloads.

F.6.3 Disk and memory sizing

Backing store requirements cannot be estimated without entity volumes and attribute data. If these items are not available persuade the members of the project team to take a view.

Double the raw data requirement to obtain the total estimated requirement. This allows for overheads such as block sizes, cylinder sizes, packing densities etc. This factor of two is applicable to non-relational DBMS; 2.5-3 should be used for relational DBMS.

Size the requirements for any other system file usage; eg logs, journals and any other relevant files. Follow the vendor's instructions which are usually available for this purpose.

If a new hardware configuration is to be used, add system requirements for the operating system, paging and swapping files, spool, libraries etc, plus any additional requirements for test and backup versions of the operating software.

Perform memory sizing by:

* using the memory size of a similar application (only if it uses the same software platform) either in this or any other organization

* using vendor's instructions, making assumptions on items such as the number of concurrent users or the number and size of virtual machines.

F.6.4 Batch systems

The method for sizing online systems can be adapted for batch systems.

In lieu of any detailed information, the Capacity Manager should attempt to identify a unit of demand, eg an account, which can be used to derive transaction frequencies where the number of overnight transactions will be 15% of the total number of accounts.

Resource profiles are derived in a similar manner to online systems. The number of I/Os needs to take into account the average number of programs that the transaction must pass through until the job(s) are completed.

Note that batch systems typically tend to be I/O, rather than CPU bound. Therefore, service levels may be constrained by the lack of I/O paths or by the sheer volume of I/Os. Every effort should be made in the design of the application to minimize the I/O traffic.

F.6.5 Detailed sizing of bespoke applications

It is typically at the logical and physical design stages that most, if not all, of the information which the Capacity Manager requires should be available.

Review the data obtained from the project team for completeness and validity prior to embarking upon the sizing exercise. In particular, check the following items:

* include data on menus (or other screen selection method). If it has been omitted then the Capacity Manager must make an allowance for the menus. Assume a 1:1 ratio between business transactions and menus, unless there is better information available

* include an allowance for the use of supervisory functions, both at the operating software and application levels. Make a small additional allowance (1% or less) in transaction frequencies to allow for any omission

* allow for the above quoted frequencies for keying or input errors (3% unless better information is available)

* validate online transaction frequencies by comparing the total against the proposed terminal population, bearing in mind how busy the system may be. This may show either that the terminal population is too small to support the estimated frequencies (question any figures which indicate rates greater than one transaction per terminal per minute). Alternatively, it may indicate that the frequencies are not high enough (eg a functionally rich system may generate far more enquiry transactions than envisaged)

* question any transaction which has a large number of logical database accesses (greater than 50) or physical I/Os (greater than 30), especially if fast response times are required.

Application sizing tools which support the target hardware and software platform can usefully be employed to calculate hardware utilizations and service levels. The following sections on CPU and I/O sizing assume that no tool is available, and therefore that the sizing must be done manually.

F.6.6 CPU sizing for online systems

The following formula can be used to estimate the CPU resource costs which will be consumed by a given transaction. It uses the basic resource costs which were discussed earlier:

$$\mathbf{CPU=C+B+P+(n_1 xLIO)+(n_2 xPIO)+(n_3 xTIO)}$$

where

CPU is the result of the formula (seconds)

C is the communications software overhead resource cost

B is the basic transaction resource cost

P is the resource cost of the estimated pathlength of source instructions, (application code) excluding DB navigation, in seconds

n_1, n_2, n_3 are the number of accesses (logical, physical or terminal respectively)

LIO is the resource cost per logical I/O

PIO is the resource cost per physical I/O

TIO is the resource cost per 1,000 characters of terminal I/O.

NOTES

* resource costs are in seconds, or fractions thereof

* P will probably be unknown since program specifications are unlikely to be available. This figure is usually only a small proportion (10-20%) of the total CPU resource cost, unless the application code is extremely complex or repetitive and is not significant. If COBOL is being used, assume for a simple transaction - 200 statements, medium - 500 statements, and complex - 1000 statements. Assuming 15 machine instructions per COBOL statement, this gives 3000, 7500 and 15000 machine instructions respectively. Then translate these figures into a resource cost, based on the power of the target CPU. On a machine that can process one million instructions per second the figures become 3, 7.5 and 15 seconds respectively

* if the size of the input/output messages are unknown assume 1000 characters for the sum of the input and output.

Enhance the formula to include logging and journalling overheads where the basic resource costs are known. Otherwise, make an allowance for such items in B (the basic resource cost of a transaction).

F.6.7 I/O sizing for online systems

If the sizing is based on a physical design, the physical I/O figures for each function should be provided by the database designer. Alternatively, if it is based on a logical design then the logical I/O must be converted to physical I/Os by the Capacity Manager. If the target DBMS has been used in a previous development, employ a logical to physical ratio based upon that experience. For example, a network database might have a ratio of 4 or 5 logical to 1 physical I/O. If there is no experience in the DBMS, seek guidance from other users of the product, or the vendor. If there is any doubt use a 1:1 ratio.

The application I/O must be supplemented by system I/O. This includes items such as page faulting, logging, journalling and any other system accesses. It is difficult to be precise on the allowance without knowing the software platform, but an allowance of 2-3 I/Os for an enquiry and 5-6 for an update transaction are useful defaults in lieu of detailed information.

Feed the results of the CPU and I/O sizings into a modelling tool to calculate hardware utilizations, service levels and the impact on existing workloads.

F.6.8 Disk space sizing

Database sizing should be performed by the database designer at the physical design stage. Add all necessary additional space requirements; eg logs, journals, system files, temporary files, test files, acceptance test files, space to perform database reorganizations. If this is a new hardware configuration, allow for all operating software requirements; eg operating system, paging and swapping files, spool, libraries etc, plus any test and backup versions of the operating system.

F.6.9 Memory sizing

Memory sizing is the most difficult aspect of capacity management and it is not possible to give precise guidelines.

The operating system requires sufficient real memory to perform its tasks in an efficient manner. This is typically called the system occupancy. Guidelines on system occupancy can usually be obtained from the hardware manufacturers.

The amount of memory which is required by an application depends on a number of variables which are unlikely to be known before coding commences; eg the size of the code, the number of terminals, the number of files, the number and size of file buffers, table requirements etc. Derive memory occupancies either from prior experience, from information which is provided by the vendor, manufacturer or other users of similar software products. It is recommended that memory sizings should err on the generous side. Any undue pressure on memory will lead to unacceptable page fault rates and a rapid degradation of performance, resulting in poor response times. Therefore avoid page faulting wherever possible. Undersizing of memory requirements has historically been a common failing.

F.6.10 Sizing batch systems

It is significantly more time-consuming to size batch systems in detail. The majority of application sizing tools are not particularly helpful in this area.

The main problems to consider are:

* can the transaction frequencies for each batch program be accurately estimated? (This may be feasible for the first program in the suite, eg it may correspond to all input and update transactions which have been entered into an online system during the day. But will the transaction frequency be known for the twenty-first program in the suite when the original data may have gone through a number of filters and only a small percentage of the original number of records have survived?)
* are resource costs available for sorts, merges and other standard utilities?
* have printing and spooling costs been considered?
* will all programs run singly in sequence?

If the answer to these questions is yes, the method which was described for online systems can be adapted for batch.

The revised CPU resource cost calculation per transaction is:

$CPU=P+(n_1 xLIO)+(n_2 xPIO)$

where

P is the estimated application pathlength

n_1 and n_2 are used to denote the number of logical I/Os and the number of physical I/Os respectively (which may be different)

LIO is the resource cost per logical I/O

PIO is the resource cost per physical I/O.

NOTE. The formula can be applied to each individual program, if detailed data is available. Alternatively, it can be applied to a job or suite of jobs, as related in the section on crude sizing for batch systems.

The comments made previously about I/O sizing for application databases (F.6.7) also apply for batch systems. However, the system accesses will be significantly less. Journalling, spool and page faulting are typically the only items which need to be accounted for. An allowance of 1-2 I/Os per transaction for updates and less than 1 for read only is typically sufficient.

Resource overheads for sorts, merges and other utilities are best derived from actual runs obtained from existing systems, or the vendor of the equipment in use, or other users of the same utilities.

Where a modelling tool is employed, incorporate the total resource costs into a model to calculate hardware utilizations and batch turnaround times.

Memory requirements for batch systems are significantly lower than for online systems, typically one megabyte or less of memory for a single batch stream. Therefore, this is unlikely to be a cause for concern overnight when little or no online work is being run. Similar comments apply to any low priority batch work which runs during the day. An allowance of 0.5Mb or less of memory should be sufficient for each batch stream. However, any high priority batch work which runs during the day may require more memory if it is to achieve the required service levels. In summary, the memory which is required for a batch stream should be sufficient to meet the agreed service levels.

F.6.11 Sizing bought-in packages

Application packages are popular alternatives to writing bespoke systems. The application packages have an impact on resource usage, and it is necessary to size the impact.

The optimum method is to obtain the individual resource profiles for each online transaction or batch job from the application package vendor, apply the transaction frequency information from the project team and feed the data into a modelling tool to calculate hardware utilizations and service levels.

Unfortunately, the majority of application package vendors tend not to provide information on resource profiles. In this situation, apply pressure to obtain all necessary information from the vendor, otherwise it is difficult to size the impact of the package. Take account of any failure on the vendor's part to supply the required information when the package is assessed during procurement. If the vendor cannot, or will not, supply the data, seek to obtain it from other existing users of the package. Finally, if all else fails, insist on organizing and running a representative benchmark to obtain the resource profiles.

Calculate disk space requirements manually by applying data volume requirements (obtained from the project team) to the standard calculations which are typically supplied by the application package vendor. Details of memory requirements are also usually supplied by the vendor.

If problems are experienced on either disk space sizing or memory requirements, seek advice from other users of the application package.

F.7 End-user computing

The use of end-user, decision support and office systems is increasing rapidly. These types of systems can be resource intensive and therefore have the capability to ruin overall performance unless they are closely monitored and controlled.

Once again, it is not easy to obtain resource profiles for such unstructured and ad hoc work. Vendors normally quote the number of users which can be supported on a given hardware configuration. Validate such claims carefully, as they are usually overly optimistic.

Perform sizing on a per-user basis. Start by categorising users, eg light, medium and heavy, where these terms indicate either frequency of use or the nature of the work. Estimate the number of concurrent users in each category. Produce a set of resource profiles for each category. Obtain resource profile data either from other existing users of the same product, or by organizing and running representative benchmarks.

Feed the information on frequencies and resource profiles into a model to calculate hardware utilizations, service levels and the impact upon existing workloads.

Annex G. Part-time capacity management

G.1 Introduction

The major assumption in this capacity management module has been that the staff resources will be available to form a section which consists of one or more full-time members. Although this is probably viable in a large or medium sized installation, it is highly improbable in a small organization. This does not mean that capacity management should be totally ignored. It means that the objectives and deliverables must be tailored to suit the local circumstances. This annex gives some ideas as to what could be attempted. Part time capacity management should not be considered as capacity management 'on the cheap'. On the contrary, considerable investment - in tools for example - will be needed. A part time Capacity Manager will most probably be under even more pressure than a full-time manager!

The assumption is that one person who has other responsibilities, usually (but not always) a systems programmer, will take on the Capacity Manager's role.

If the organization is to have any chance of success, the following points must be noted:

* communication is even more important in this environment, especially maximum forewarning of major changes which are planned
* it is imperative that the appointed person is able to manage their time effectively. Unfortunately in this situation, capacity management is often tackled only when other duties permit. This means that it is neglected and becomes crisis management. The only solution is to plan the time and duration of effort which must be put into capacity management
* effective use must be made of tools. However, remember that modelling is not capacity management. The tools can be extremely useful, and they can save time, but they are only tools. They do not obviate the need for human effort, especially in the assessment of the results
* the person will be unable to perform all necessary tasks. Some of the duties will need to be performed by other IT personnel. For example, information on business growth may be supplied by IT management.

The following paragraphs discuss work which may be performed in each element of capacity management.

G.2 Performance management

The objective in Performance Management should be to minimize the amount of effort which is required to monitor current performance. This can be achieved by the judicious use of exception reports which highlight when thresholds are approached or exceeded. There are some products in the IBM and ICL marketplaces which address this area. Otherwise, the effort required to develop these reports will more than pay for itself.

Regular management reports can be limited to overall CPU (OCP), page fault (VSI), and I/O rates and disk space usage. Break the figures down further into TP, timesharing and batch if time permits.

G.3 Workload management

The Capacity Manager is unlikely to be able to devote the necessary time to workload forecasting. It is recommended that the Change Manager assumes the responsibility to gather the required information from the users as part of their normal liaison. This information will form the input to the production of the capacity plan.

G.4 Capacity plan

Modelling tools will greatly assist the process of producing the plan. Products which allow full details of the proposed plan to be input at one time and subsequently evaluated with no operator intervention, are advantageous in this environment. It is probable that a technical-style report will be delivered by the Capacity Manager to IT management. The actual plan which goes to senior management should be produced by the IT Services Manager.

G.5 Service level management

It is unlikely that service level agreements will be viable in this scenario. If IT management do not have the utmost confidence that service levels can be achieved and maintained then it is recommended that objectives, rather than agreements, are employed.

G.6 Application sizing

Application sizing will probably suffer more than any other area. Sizing can be done on the basis of 'it looks like this existing system', but only when the manager is confident that this is indeed the case. If time and/or expertise does not permit the planner to size the proposed application satisfactorily, and it is felt that the application may have a major impact on the installation, consider the use of external resources to perform this work.

Application sizing tools may be beneficial: if they can be used to model the proposed hardware/software platform, if they allow crude sizings to be performed with a minimum of effort, and if the input data is available from the developers. If the answer to any these questions is no, the use of such tools may be counter-productive.

G.7 Cost management

For Cost Management, it will only be necessary to ensure that sufficient accounting data is available for costing/chargeback purposes. Costing work will normally be carried out by a part-time Cost Manager in this environment.

G.8 Resource management

Finally, Resource Management should be tackled in conjunction with Operations. They should be responsible for the configuration aspects with any necessary assistance provided by the Capacity Manager.

Annex H. Distributed systems

H.1 Distributed system

A distributed system is defined as a system where the data and computing power is dispersed over a number of host computers which are usually sited in separate geographic locations. The majority of the data which needs to be accessed will be held on the user's local computer but there may be occasions where the required data, eg corporate rather than site-specific data, is held on one of the other computers in the network. Distributed systems allow access to these 'remote' computers in a manner which is totally transparent to the user. Figure H.1 provides an example of a distributed transaction for an Enquiry.

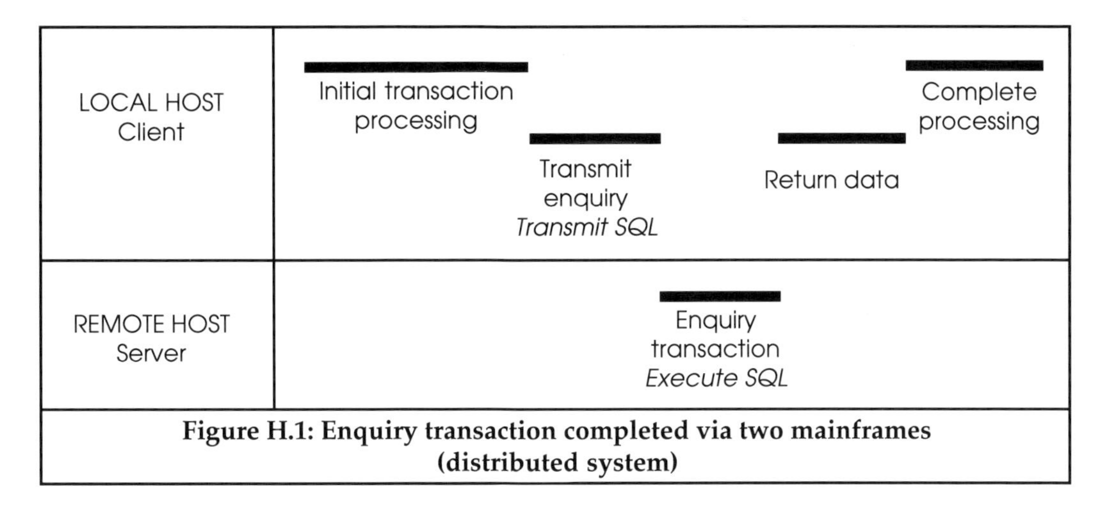

Figure H.1: Enquiry transaction completed via two mainframes (distributed system)

H.2 Organization

In terms of capacity management organization, there are two main options. The recommended approach is that a single Capacity Manager is appointed, preferably with one team, to have overall capacity management responsibility for the total network of computers and communications equipment. The alternative approach is to have separate Capacity Managers and capacity management teams at each location. This latter approach is not recommended since it may lead to the production of conflicting results, particularly in the areas of workload forecasting, predicted service levels and capacity plans.

H.3 Performance management

Performance Management tasks must take place on each individual host computer since it will be necessary to optimize the performance of each machine. Tuning should ensure that accessing of remote machines is kept to an absolute minimum since this activity involves the use of additional resources and will have an adverse impact on response times. For example, the replication of reference data on each computer instead of a centrally held set will reduce resource consumption and improve response times, although this solution may cause problems on updating the reference data at each site.

The information in H.1, H.2 and H.3 is also broadly applicable to client-server systems.

H.4 Tuning

Tuning may involve investigation of the complete system. For example, it may be desirable, if it is feasible, to re-distribute the data in order that performance bottlenecks on one machine may be resolved by moving the overheads to another machine which has spare capacity. This may avoid the need for hardware upgrades by smoothing resource usage over the entire system. However, there is a concomitant effect of raising the network traffic levels. Thus a computer bottleneck may be replaced by a network bottleneck. Careful modelling of the proposed redistribution is therefore essential.

The complete network will be viewed as a single entity from a performance monitoring and tuning aspect.

One part of Workload Management involves the Capacity Manager developing an understanding of the systems which run on the hardware of each individual host. Once this is understood the capacity planner must take into account the volume of transactions which are transmitted to/from other hosts. They can usually be identified either by transaction name (where particular transaction(s) are set up to deal with transmission functions), or by the network name which may actually be the identity of the sending/receiving host rather than a terminal identifier, or by a mailbox name.

H.5 Resource profiles

The calculation of resource profiles on each individual host should include the resource overheads which are incurred in the transmission process.

Workload forecasting can be more difficult to handle on distributed systems, particularly when attempting to identify the user(s). It would be preferable if there was a single user who could describe the future requirements for the entire organization. Unfortunately, this is not always possible. If the Capacity Manager has to liaise with different Users at separate geographic locations then interviewing may be difficult. Therefore, the Capacity Manager may need to use proformae which are distributed to the users. A pragmatic solution to this problem may be to visit a percentage of the users each quarter but rely on proformae for the remainder, attempting to visit each user at least once a year.

Forecast calculations should be performed for the entire organization and for each individual host system. When converting business requirements into transaction frequencies the Capacity Manager must make suitable allowance for the volume of transactions which are transmitted into/out of each host system. The number of transactions which require to be transmitted can be derived from observation of historical trends unless better information is available from the users.

It is frequently the case with distributed systems (particularly as PC workstations become more powerful and widespread, and with the increased use of LAN file servers) that the network capacity required for transaction processing is smaller than that required for file transfer. File transfer is typically carried out overnight to reconcile and update the distributed data and software. Careful planning of data distribution is essential to avoid running out of network capacity and/or transmission time.

Note that because of the volumes involved, it is still not uncommon for data distribution to be carried out via diskettes in the post. Such a technique, while avoiding network saturation has attendant problems for change management.

H.6 Application sizing

Application sizing for distributed systems must be performed separately for each host. To perform this task the Capacity Manager will require additional information. For transaction frequencies by business function the following will be required:

* the number of transactions which will be performed locally
* the number of transactions that will be transmitted to another host
* the number of transactions that will be received from other hosts
* the volume of data to be transmitted.

If no information is available on the volume of transactions and data which are transmitted, use any historical data which may be available from existing systems or use a 'rule of thumb' figure of 10% for transactions which are transmitted and 10% for the number that are received.

Also, additional details of the required database accessing may have to be provided, showing those accesses which will be performed on another host if the transaction is transferred, so that they can be excluded from the calculations for the local host.

Distributed systems use more resources than non-distributed systems, particularly CPU, due to the extra work involved in transferring transactions (TP Monitor and communications software) and the spawning of additional transactions to process the transferred transactions. The Capacity Manager must include these additional resources in the sizing calculations. Historical data from existing systems may be used to calculate the resource overheads which are incurred for distributed systems. In lieu of any data a rule of thumb increase in the order of 30-40% should be added to the total resources which are calculated.

H.7 Modelling

Modelling brings additional problems to the Capacity Manager. Firstly, it will be necessary to model each host separately. Secondly, the total response time at the terminal for distributed transactions will be the sum of two sets of network response time and two sets of host response time as shown in Figure H.2. (True also for client-server architectures).

PROCESS						
Input from terminal	Start local processing	Transmit transaction	Run remote transaction	Return data	Complete local processing	Send output to terminal
NETWORK	HOST (LOCAL)	NETWORK	HOST (REMOTE)	NETWORK	HOST (LOCAL)	NETWORK
RESPONSE TIME						

Figure H2: Components making up response time of enquiry transaction completed via two mainframes (distributed system)

The Capacity Manager should attempt, where possible, to keep transferred transactions separate from local transactions in a model since the latter will typically use more resources; this may distort the model response times if they are amalgamated, giving a higher total response time for the transferred transactions and a lower one for the local transactions. The separation can be achieved by defining them as discrete workloads within a model.

When the Capacity Manager is modelling prior to producing a capacity plan he/she should be attempting to optimize performance against cost over the total system. For example, data may be moved from one host to another in order to smooth performance problems but this may only be done if it does not adversely affect service levels or cause operational problems. In addition, the Capacity Manager should investigate any beneficial effects which may be obtained by the redeployment of hardware, usually CPUs between sites. For example, if a replacement CPU is required at one site it might be advantageous to move the old CPU to one of the other sites to provide more power at that site. The Capacity Manager can also investigate downsizing, ie replacing the central host with distributed minis/PCs.

A separate, detailed Capacity Plan should be produced for each host. In addition, a summary plan document should be produced for management which amalgamates the hardware requirements and cost implications from these individual plans.

Annex I. Resource cost factors for different software platforms

If the Capacity Manager is sizing a new application which will be based on a software platform for which he/she has no information then the following (Figure I.1) rule of thumb conversion factor figures may be useful in helping to derive some rough resource profiles from data on existing systems. See also Figure J.2.

Figure I.1: Rule of thumb conversion factors

Platform	CPU Factor	I/O Factor
3GL and flat files	1	1
3GL and hierarchical DBMS	1.2-1.5	1.2-1.5
3GL and CODASYL DBMS	1.7-2.0	1.5-2.0
4GL and hierarchical DBMS	1.5-2.0	1.5-1.8
4GL and CODASYL DBMS	1.8-2.3	1.8-2.0
4GL and Relational DBMS	2.5-3.0	2.0-2.5

For example, if a transaction which is written in a 3GL (COBOL) with flat files uses 100 milliseconds of CPU and performs 6 I/Os, the equivalent transaction in a 4GL with a CODASYL database may consume 200 milliseconds of CPU and perform 12 I/Os.

These relative performance factors should be used with great care. For example, the implementation of a 4GL with a relational database can consume less resources than the table indicates, particularly if it is severely limited in its use of relational features. Alternatively, the same type of system may use much higher resources than those indicated in the table, particularly if it makes free use of relational features such as joins and full table scans. Always use actual monitored figures wherever possible. Only resort to these factors when all else fails.

Annex J elaborates further on the problems surrounding new applications particularly in relation to Greenfield sites.

Annex J. Capacity & performance problems in greenfield sites

The advice which has been given in this module is also relevant to greenfield sites, ie where there is no existing computer facility. However, the order in which the individual elements of capacity management are tackled will differ.

J.1 Introduction

If the procurement for the hardware has not commenced the initial task may be to size the hardware which will be required to support the projected workload. Therefore, the procurement of host and network modelling tools should be considered immediately to assist this task.

There is an ideal opportunity to establish Service Level Management from the outset. The results of the sizing exercises will provide the initial input to the establishment of the first SLAs.

J.2 Initial sizing

The complete sizing should cater for the expected volumes for a minimum of two years for the initial applications, plus the future implementation of any additional applications which may be implemented over that period of time. The results of the sizing exercise should be put into an initial capacity plan document which should be used in the procurement process.

In the situation where a turnkey solution is being provided by a software house the Capacity Manager should check the sizing calculations to ensure that he/she is satisfied that sufficient hardware has been configured to meet the total requirement.

J.3 Pre-installation

Any time which is available between the initial sizing and the commissioning of the hardware should be used to do as much of the design work (and development work, if access is available to a suitable computer) for capacity management as possible. In particular, Service Level Monitoring plus CDB development and Reporting should be progressed as soon as possible.

In addition, an embryonic workload catalogue can be created from the information that is currently available.

J.4 Post-installation

Performance Management should be implemented as soon as the hardware has been commissioned even if there is some delay before the first production applications are implemented, usually because they are being developed on the target hardware. CDB and Reporting should be implemented as soon as possible after the commissioning process.

The service level monitoring system should preferably be implemented when the first production application goes live, or as soon after as possible. Regular workload forecasting should commence approximately two months after the first implementation.

The next capacity plan should be scheduled to fit in with the business planning cycle.

J.5 Total Acquisition Process (TAP)

CCTA is currently finalising details of what is to be known as the Total Acquisition Process (TAP). Procurement of hardware will in future be governed by the detailed TAP.

Clearly, the TAP should include sizing and capacity considerations: some work has been carried out on how best to embrace all of the activities and requirements of capacity management within the TAP. The following guidance has been distilled from CCTA involvement with capacity problems in Government.

J.6 The approach

An approach is required based on the assumptions that the workload cannot be sufficiently well defined for sizing purposes and that capacity requirements cannot be predetermined.

It is best to assume that the initial combination of new systems and applications will be unlikely to meet performance requirements and tuning and/or enhancements will be necessary. With this in mind, clearly a standard high level sizing methodology should be introduced to ensure consistency in proposals and to identify anomalies during development. This should be integrated with system development, project management and risk assessment methodologies.

J.7 Workload definitions

It is assumed that sufficient information can be provided in an Operational Requirement (OR) specification to enable suppliers to carry out accurate sizing.

Two examples of mandatory requirements on processing capacity and on-line storage from an actual OR are:

> "The processing capacity of the system must be sufficient to deal with a peak transaction rate of 3850 per hour, assuming 4 message pairs per transaction and 95% response times of 5 seconds or less", and

> "The size of the on-line disc storage devices must be based on using only 75% of their capacity for the total estimated 1500 Mbytes of raw storage required".

These represent fine principles for extending known applications but are solution-based in the assumptions used for message pairs per transaction and disk capacity parameters.

For new database applications, sizing usually has to be based on SSADM tables of logical transaction volumes and database entities. For sizing purposes, additional information is required for application and solution-based assumptions, on:

* message pairs per transaction
* the number of disk I/Os
* communications traffic.

For disk capacity calculations, application and solution-based assumptions have to be made on record sizes and any indexing requirements.

Experience indicates that there can be a 3 to 1 or greater variation between proposals in converting logical attributes to physical attributes required for sizing purposes. With naive suppliers, the classic mistake is to interpret transactions as message pairs, an obvious problem which suggests that a formalized sizing methodology is required.

For office system applications, the situation can be much worse as the definition of much of the workload volumes is not produced by a design methodology.

J.8 Application efficiency impact

As reflected in J.13, the use of 4GLs can be expected to increase resource demands by a factor of 3, compared with COBOL. In turn, the latter may demand 3 times the capacity of Assembler programs. A greater problem, with 4GLs, is the tendency for the software to produce complex enquiries, searches and reports from apparently simple statements input by the user. It also appears to be far too easy to produce inefficient code and poor system design leading to excessive resource demands.

J.9 Risk assessment factors

Examination of the margins of error possible in sizing gives an indication of the risks involved and highlights the reasons for treating sizing and capacity in a different way for a successful Total Acquisition Process.

Figure J.1 represents a range of multiplication factors for risk assessment.

Figure J.1: Multiplication factors

RISK RANGE	
User specified logical volumes	1 to 3
Supplier conversion to physical volumes	1 to 3
Sizing parameters used	1 to 3
Application efficiency	1 to 10

Although figure J.1 indicates that up to 270 times (if all of the top range figures are multiplied) more resources than expected might be required, using mid-range expectations, the figure reduces to 40 times (2x2x2x5) the initially expected resources, still an extremely large risk factor. If an accurate CRAMM exercise was carried out to assess sizing and capacity risks, enhancement potential would become one of the major evaluation criteria.

Additionally, there is a high risk that individual users will exploit the facilities in, initially, unspecified ways, which will further increase resource demands.

J.10 Other performance considerations

As well as the sizing difficulties described, there are a number of other performance considerations that are becoming more important with advanced technology. For example, office system response time requirements are generally specified in the same way as for TP systems: anyone who has used a system will realize that obtaining 95% of response times within 4 seconds, from 'Execute' to the first character of the next screen (perhaps an intermediate message) being displayed, does not reflect acceptable performance.

A second example which might apply in Executive Agencies is where screen operators' pay is dependent on productivity. When response times are too long, (slowing down data entry) something needs to be done quickly. This may well be a requirement in future procurement procedures.

J.11 The future

Present procurement procedures do not adequately deal with the realities of performance, sizing and capacity. Changes are required covering financing of enhancements, application tuning, development activity, consistent approaches to sizing and evaluation methods.

If organizations are prepared to embrace the assumption that hardware is relatively cheap (and accepting that initial estimates of capacity requirement are unlikely to be accurate and probably always on the low side) procurement procedures must embrace the concept that application tuning and/or system enhancements will be required before the system goes live. As mentioned in the management summary, hardware costs may be falling but capacity management remains necessary if the organization wishes to obtain value for money and to ensure the right amount of capacity is always available.

It would seem appropriate therefore to split the development budget into two, covering development and optimization separately. During the optimization phase, assuming that a case can be made to show that tuning would be the most expensive option, it should be possible to justify system enhancements.

Formalized procedures could be included within the Project Plan to embrace performance, sizing and capacity considerations, including optimization of the design and application software. Specific activities would be required for refining the sizing and verifying capacity requirements. To this end, a performance sub-project should be created with a Performance Assurance Coordinator responsible for reporting progress to the Project Board.

J.12 Sizing methodology

A simple sizing methodology could be used, covering all stages from specification to live operation. There may be a need for complex modelling and measurement but the results should be used to update the output which will identify the capacity demands of each application, overall capacity utilization and response times. The methodology recommended is based on using spreadsheets as shown in J.13. The following examples demonstrate how they can be used for new database applications. A different approach may be suitable when extending existing applications and a variation used when considering office systems.

J.12.1 Feasibility study

During the feasibility study, initial estimates of the range and complexity of applications should be obtained along with estimates of transaction rates or numbers of concurrent users by application. Approximations of capacity requirements can be obtained by using rules of thumb such as those given in J.13. Response time estimates can be derived from the same source to verify that the minimum capacity identified appears to have sufficient speed to meet reasonable requirements.

As shown in the examples in J.13, application design constraints may be identified, for example regarding disk I/Os or memory capacity.

Processor MIPS ratings can be obtained from a CCTA product and performance database, which covers present systems and many future expectations.

J.12.2 Mini proposal

The statement of requirement could include a spreadsheet definition (on a floppy disk) with logical transaction volumes and database entities derived directly from SSADM.

The suppliers will need to enter their estimates of:

* message pairs per transaction
* disk and communications I/Os
* system overheads,

in order to calculate utilization figures. They will also have to enter estimated:

* CPU times
* disk I/Os
* communications traffic
* queueing factors
* percentile multipliers,

in order to estimate response times.

A second spreadsheet could be used to show database entities. The supplier would need to enter:

* logical to physical conversion factors
* record sizes
* indexing overheads
* other overheads,

in order to estimate disk capacity. A cross-check should be made between the number of disk drives suggested for capacity reasons and the number suggested in utilization calculations.

A third spreadsheet, covering memory capacity, might also be needed. The supplier would need to indicate demands by the:

* operating system
* application software
* overheads
    - by connected users and devices
    - by active users and applications,

identifying separately any data buffering requirements. The latter is an area often omitted.

Although the sizings are most unlikely to be very accurate, a standardized approach has the following advantages:

* the consistent approach enables easy comparisons
* suppliers who lack knowledge of the impact of different applications, or who do not have performance expertise, will be identified
* the methodology will identify design constraints of particular solutions, for example, communications loading could be significant (at least different) with a client server architecture
* the calculations may identify certain performance or capacity attributes that can be made contractual.

J.12.3 Shortlisted suppliers

The procedures at this stage will be the same as above but there may be more up-to-date volumetrics. However, emphasis should be placed on the suppliers providing justification for the sizing parameters used.

In order to demonstrate that future enhancements will be adequate and available, a range of sizings should be requested, covering extremes of volumetrics, physical volume conversion factors, sizing parameters and assumptions of application code efficiency. This provides input to a risk analysis study.

If performance demonstrations or benchmark runs are required, the results should be incorporated in the spreadsheet and attempts made to justify sizing parameters used. If facilities demonstrations are required, the opportunity should be taken to consider performance and capacity by noting response times or requesting performance monitoring information.

J.12.4 Application development

The main reason for having a performance sub-project is to match the application capacity demands to the speed of the supplied hardware and software, based on acknowledgement that initial sizings are unlikely to be correct. Specific milestones should be identified, where capacity demands and performance are reassessed and the Project Assurance Coordinator is required to report to the Project Board:

* when volumetric physical attributes are determined to assess the impact of real message pairs and physical I/Os

* during the database and application design phase where confirmation is required that sizing assumptions still apply
* when transactions are implemented. Firstly, response times on an otherwise empty or lightly loaded system can be noted, followed by others under different loading conditions. Secondly, a method of measuring the CPU, I/O and communication demands should be determined and measurements made
* during application testing when specific multi-user tests should be carried out with performance monitoring enabled
* during a system testing phase, with real users carrying out reasonably well defined activities
* in the event of volumes being revised.

A post-implementation review will also be required to determine whether and where redesign or tuning is required or whether a case should be made for enhancements.

J.13 Sizing rules of thumb

The following 'rules of thumb' (Figure J.2, overleaf) are based on practical experience, obtained during performance investigations, and from information supplied by IBM and ICL. For CPU requirements, different MIPS per user figures are given for mainframes, minicomputers and RISC based UNIX systems as the MIPS speed ratings are generally derived from completely different sources.

The MIPS/USER figures relate to 1 message pair per minute per user. The average for 4GL applications could be 1.5 per minute per user or 2 to 3 per minute per user for light applications.

The MIPS/USER figures are based on a 70% CPU utilization. Thus the equivalent number of instructions involved, as used in estimating CPU time for response time calculations, is:

Millions of instructions = 60 x MIPS/USER x 0.7.

Thus, 0.1 and 1.33 MIPS per user equate to 4.2 and 55.9 millions of instructions which, on a 10 MIPS system, indicate 0.42 and 5.6 seconds of CPU time.

APPLICATION	CPU MIPS PER USER MAINFRAME	MINI	RISC UNIX	MEMORY 5 MB+ MB/USR	DISK DRIVES/ USER
RDB/4GL general	0.1	0.2	0.4	1.0	0.1
RDB/4GL light	0.03	0.07	0.15	0.75	0.05
RDB/4GL heavy	0.33	0.67	1.33	4.0	0.4
DB/3GL general	0.03	0.07	0.15		
DB/Assembler	0.01	0.02	0.04		
OA General	0.1	0.2	0.4	0.5	0.1
Light WP	0.03	0.07	0.15	0.5	0.05
Heavy OA	0.33	0.67	1.33	2.0	0.2
Batch Jobs	0.5	1.0	2.0	4.0	0.5
4GL Development	0.33	0.67	1.33	4.0	0.4

Figure J.2: Sizing rules of thumb

The disk figures are based on 40% utilization and 30 milliseconds average access time or 13.33 I/Os per second per drive. The number of disk I/Os per message pair is:

Disk I/Os per message pair = 60 x DISKS/USER x 13.33

Thus, 0.05 and 0.4 disks per user equate to 40 to 320 I/Os or average service times of 1.2 and 9.6 seconds. In practice one would hope that the number of I/Os per message pair could be reduced to less than 10.

Logical transactions to message pairs	x 2 to 10
Logical I/Os to physical I/Os It could be less than 1 with clever memory buffering	x 2 to 8
Database memory data buffer	2% of DB size
RDB Indexes	15%-25% DB size
Busy hour up to	0.33 busy day.

Response time calculations

Examples of calculating minimum CPU and disk times are given above. It is useful to measure response times on a lightly loaded system to confirm that they are of the right order of magnitude. As the loads build up, queues form and the average response times increase. The following is derived from a CCTA-produced spreadsheet model, and gives an indication of the queueing factors for 1 to 4 CPUs at 50% to 80% utilization.

Total CPU Utilization	50%	60%	70%	80%
1 CPU	2.0	2.5	3.3	5.0
2 CPU	1.5	1.7	2.0	2.8
4 CPU	1.2	1.3	1.5	1.7

Unless there is significant disk channel contention, leading to missed disk revolutions, the factor for disks should normally be in the range 1.1 to 1.5.

For example, a single CPU at 70% utilization and disk factor 1.2 with nominal CPU and I/O time of 0.42 and 1.2 seconds:

CPU average response time = 0.42 x 3.3 = 1.39 seconds

Disk average response time = 1.2 x 1.2 = 1.44 seconds

System average response time = 2.83 seconds

Percentile response times are more difficult to measure and predict. Extended response times can be caused by peaks in the random arrival of transactions, periodic high priority system activity, resource contention eg database deadlocks and variation in the impact of the particular class of message pair being considered. Ninety-five percentile response times can be 3 to 5 times the mean and 90 pecentiles 2 to 4 times the mean.

J.14 Initial sizing spreadsheet

Specified by user..... Supplier Estimates.....Calculated Loading

Trans-action	Type	Peak hr volumes	MsPr/ trans	Load/ CPU	Load/ Disks	MsPr comms	Total CPU	Load disks	Comms
Trans1	L Updt	240	3	0.2	30	5	144	21600	3600
Trans2	M Updt	200	3	0.3	40	5	180	24000	3000
Trans3	H Updt	150	3	0.4	50	5	180	22500	2250
Trans4	L Enq	350	3	0.2	15	5	210	15750	5250
Trans5	M Enq	300	3	0.2	25	5	180	22500	4500
Trans6	H Enq	200	3	0.3	35	5	180	21000	3000
Trans7	L Trce	100	3	0.4	75	5	120	22500	1500
Trans8	M Trce	80	3	0.6	150	5	144	36000	1200
Trans8	H Trce	60	3	0.9	200	5	162	36000	900
Sub-Total							1500	221850	25200
System Overheads							300	10000	
Disk Service Time								0.025	
Total Time							1800	5796	
% Utilization							50.0	161.0	
Number of Units							1	8	
Utilization/Unit							50.0	20.1	

RESPONSE TIME ESTIMATES

Queueing Factor			95% Factor	
CPU	Dsk	Com	Sys	Com
2.0	1.1	2.0	3.0	5.0

Message Pair	Minimum Time				Mean Response Secs				95% Response		
	CPU	Dsk	Com	Tot	CPU	Dsk	Com	Tot	Sys	Com	Tot
L Updt	0.2	0.8	0.5	1.5	0.4	0.8	1.0	2.2	3.7	5.0	6.2
M Updt	0.3	1.0	0.5	1.8	0.6	1.1	1.0	2.7	5.1	5.0	7.1
H Updt	0.4	1.3	0.5	2.2	0.8	1.4	1.0	3.2	6.5	5.0	8.2
L Enq	0.2	0.4	0.5	1.1	0.4	0.4	1.0	1.8	2.4	5.0	5.6
M Enq	0.2	0.6	0.5	1.3	0.4	0.7	1.0	2.1	3.3	5.0	6.0
H Enq	0.3	0.9	0.5	1.7	0.6	1.0	1.0	2.6	4.7	5.0	6.9
L Trce	0.4	1.9	0.5	2.8	0.8	2.1	1.0	3.9	8.6	5.0	9.9
M Trce	0.6	3.8	0.5	4.9	1.2	4.1	1.0	6.3	16.0	5.0	16.7
H Trce	0.9	5.0	0.5	6.4	1.8	5.5	1.0	8.3	21.9	5.0	22.5

Annex K. Microcomputers

K.1 Introduction

Microcomputers represent a challenge to Capacity Managers since their capacity management is not straightforward. The IT Infrastructure Library module **Management of Local Processors and Terminals** should be consulted for background knowledge about the subject. The reason for this difficulty is that these systems do not typically provide any performance monitoring data at the present time. Therefore, any monitoring will tend to rely upon observation and tuning is likely to be based on empirical methods, rather than hard facts. Hence, it is essential that due consideration is given to the initial selection of equipment in order that performance problems may be pre-empted, wherever possible.

The following sections outline the performance issues which should be considered prior to the initial procurement or upgrading of micro-based hardware.

It should be noted that the microcomputers market is subject to constant change and that therefore the comments which are made in the sections below reflect the current situation.

K.2 CPUs

Microcomputers are typically based on Motorola, Intel or Intel-licensed chips. For example, the Macintosh uses the Motorola 68000 chip, while IBM-compatible PCs employ the Intel or Intel-licensed chip.

Many of the PCs which are in operation today are IBM compatibles which run MS-DOS. They typically have either the 16-bit Intel 80286 chip or the 32-bit Intel 80386. The 80286 operates at speeds from 6Mhz to 16Mhz, whereas the 80386 can run at 16-33Mhz. The 80386SX is a variant of the 80386, being identical in software functionality but slightly slower in performance, albeit cheaper.

Faster chips should be considered for processor intensive applications such as modelling or CASE tools, high resolution graphics, workstations, any windowing environment or file servers.

Maths co-processors are available which can speed up mathematical operations. However, a check should be carried out to ensure that the proposed software application(s) can make use of such processors.

Intel 80486 systems are now available but typically in the form of multi-user systems.

K.3 Memory

The major concern in the area of memory management relates to MS-DOS based systems. MS-DOS based machines have been restricted to using 640Kb of main memory, in which both the operating system and the user program have to run. Memory immediately above this, the 384Kb up to 1Mb, was reserved for system use.

Over the past few years this has become a barrier to software developers and users alike, with the move towards larger more complex programs and co-residency (though not multitasking) of programs. The use of terminate and stay resident programs (TSRs) such as Sidekick, device drivers for LANs and communications software may mean that the application software does not fit into 640Kb.

There have been a number of developments to allow the use of additional memory. This subject is quite complex and the market has not yet stabilized. The capacity planner may need to consider the following options if there is insufficient memory.

'Extended memory' allows programs which run in protected mode to access memory above 1Mb directly, up to 16Mb on the 80286 and 4 gigabytes on the 80386. This facility can only be used by specially constructed software packages. Note that MS-DOS is a real-mode operating system and cannot use extended memory directly. The use of a 'DOS Extender' is typically required to make effective use of extended memory. DOS Extenders (eg Rational Systems DOS/16M) enable software to run in protected mode, and thus be able to use extended memory, while still having the ability to access DOS devices and services.

80386-based PCs have another method for using more memory, 'virtual 8086' mode. This facility allows the PC to support many MS-DOS applications simultaneously, each in what appears to be the first 1Mb of memory. Windows/386, Concurrent DOS 386 and DESQview/386 use this facility to provide some degree of multi-program residency or multi-user systems.

A third option is to use 'Expanded memory' (as per the Lotus/Intel/ Microsoft Expanded Memory Specification - LIM EMS). This employs memory above 1Mb by transferring pages of memory into an area between 640Kb and 1Mb, which can then be directly accessed by MS-DOS and its applications. Once again, application software must be written to support expanded memory.

Another approach for 80286-based machines is the use of a hardware device called Chargecard which effectively frees memory between 640Kb and 1Mb. Microsoft's Windows 3 is another approach.

Operating systems such as OS/2, Unix and the Macintosh operating system do not have such artificial memory constraints. OS/2 can support up to 16 megabytes, Unix up to 4 gigabytes and the current Macintosh architecture 8 megabytes.

K.4 Disks

The currently available hard disks vary in capacity from 20 to several hundred megabytes. Average disk service times for an I/O are typically in the range of 30-50ms which are comparable to the times which can be obtained on many minicomputers.

Optical disks (or WORMs) may be considered suitable for applications where very large read-only databases are required. Note that the average disk service times for these devices are significantly larger than the time for Winchester disks, typically in the range 150-500ms.

Disk bottlenecks are the most common performance problems which are encountered on micro-based systems, frequently caused by fragmentation of files. There are some utilities available, eg Norton Utilities for MS-DOS, which will consolidate data into a single contiguous area. In addition, through the use of these utilities, frequently used files can be positioned at the beginning of the disk to minimize head movement.

On multi-user systems a single disk may become a bottleneck, therefore the use of multiple hard disks should be considered where this is possible.

In addition, the use of small directories and well organized tree structures will improve speed of access.

The use of RAM (or cache) disks which use memory rather than disk can also greatly improve performance. However, they should only be used for read-only files since the data will be lost if the system crashes.

The separation of software and data into separate directories will make back-ups quicker since only the data usually requires regular back-up.

K.5 Tape drives

Tape drives are mostly used to back up large amounts of data. Tape capacities are typically in the range of 50-200mb. In addition to capacity, I/O service times are important. Generally, only true streaming devices are fast enough for large back-ups.

K.6 Printers

The throughput of print devices may be improved by the following considerations:

* use of parallel rather than serial interface
* choice of connecting cable and flow control protocol
* use of cartridge/resident fonts rather than downloaded fonts
* the use of internal print buffers
* the capabilities of laser-printing technology.

K.7 Communications

The subject of **Network Management** is covered in the appropriate IT Infrastructure Library module and this should be consulted for background information.

Facilities are available to connect individual microcomputers to a LAN or a remote host. The following should be considered, particularly where large file transfers are contemplated via remote links:

* line speed supported
* use of data compaction protocols.

Note that the implications of a connection to a remote LAN in order to access the data on a file server should be carefully considered. The service time per I/O will be very high due to the additional time which will be taken to transfer blocks across the WAN (wide area network).

K.8 LANs

The general philosophy behind the configuration of LANs is the ability to share resources such as disks and printers. The two main types of LAN which should be considered are Ethernet and Token Ring. Both types require network adaptor cards in the PC or workstation.

The major performance problems on LANs tend to be caused by bottlenecks on the disk file server. Such bottlenecks may be circumvented by considering:

* judicious use of the shared disk facility. Where possible, the data should be held locally, thus obviating the need to use the file server. The disadvantages of this approach may be that it becomes more of a chore to take back-ups and it may be more expensive to have individual copies of software rather than a networked copy
* the use of multiple disk devices on any single fileserver station
* the use of multiple file servers
* minimization of head movement and the general optimization of disk performance, as discussed in C.1.3.

Where communications are required to a remote system, the use of a dedicated communications server (gateway) which is capable of supporting multiple sessions and possibly multiple connections should be considered. Use of such a server should increase the capabilities of individual workstations.

Some LANs, which allow the incorporation of duplicate hardware which may be switched in if a failure occurs, may be appropriate for critical applications.

K.9 Other capacity planning issues

Other capacity planning issues include:

* requirement to have sufficient terminals to meet typical and peak levels of user demand. In addition, a degree of redundancy may assist in the attainment of SLAs
* ease of expansion is an important issue as the need to connect to other IT systems becomes ever greater
* the Capacity Manager should consult the Network Manager with reference to the possible siting of equipment
* long running, LAN resource intensive tasks should be run out of normal office hours wherever possible.

Annex L. Examples of capacity management reports

L.1 Contents

Figures on pages L2 to L7 are examples of reports for the current period.

Figures on pages L8 to L12 are examples of reports which show historical trends.

Figures on pages L13 to L17 are examples of forecasts created by modelling packages.

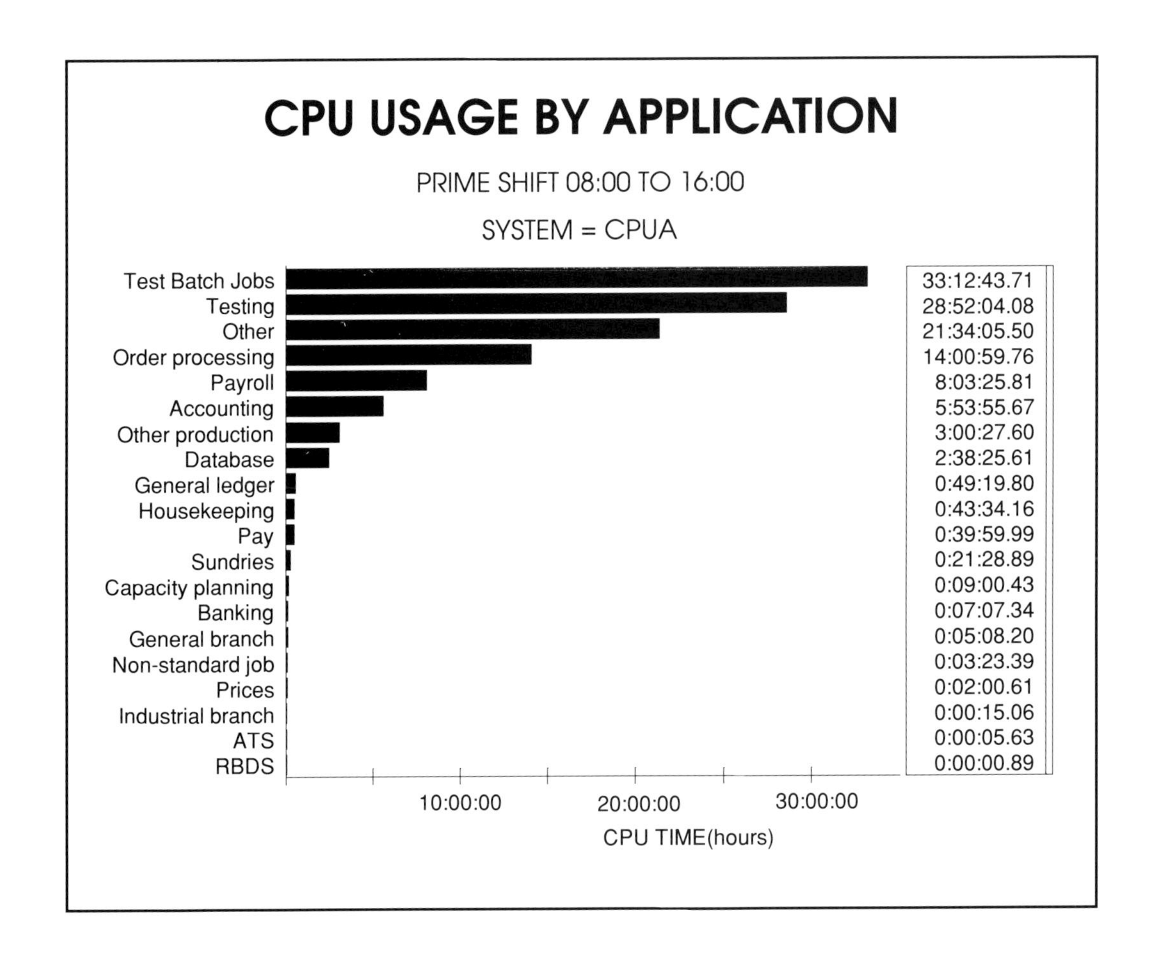
CPU USAGE BY APPLICATION
PRIME SHIFT 08:00 TO 16:00
SYSTEM = CPUA
Test Batch Jobs
Testing
Other
Order processing
Payroll
Accounting
Other production
Database
General ledger
Housekeeping
Pay
Sundries
Capacity planning
Banking
General branch
Non-standard job
Prices
Industrial branch
ATS
RBDS
33:12:43.71
28:52:04.08
21:34:05.50
14:00:59.76
8:03:25.81
5:53:55.67
3:00:27.60
2:38:25.61
0:49:19.80
0:43:34.16
0:39:59.99
0:21:28.89
0:09:00.43
0:07:07.34
0:05:08.20
0:03:23.39
0:02:00.61
0:00:15.06
0:00:05.63
0:00:00.89
10:00:00
20:00:00
30:00:00
CPU TIME(hours)

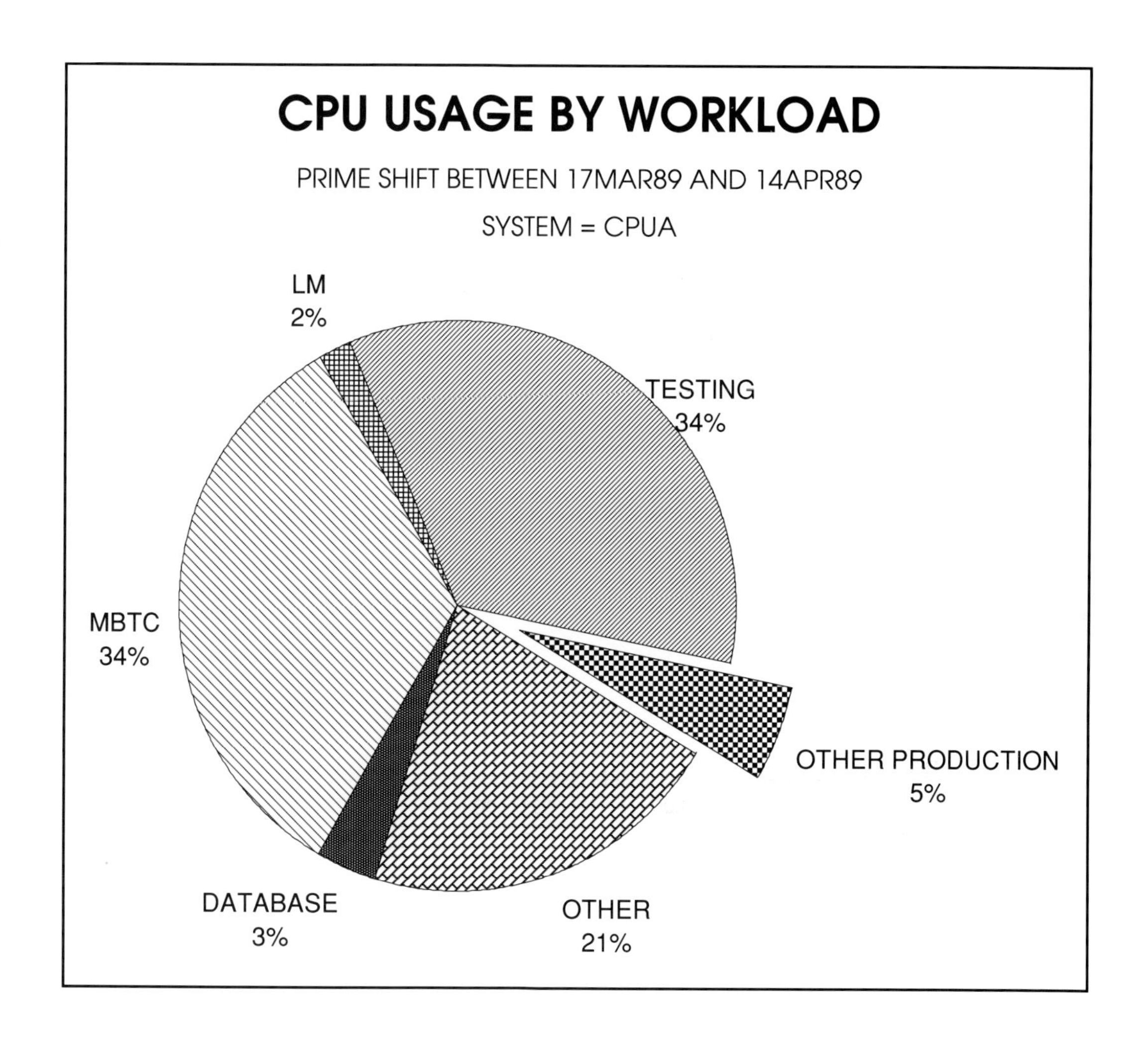
CPU USAGE BY WORKLOAD
PRIME SHIFT BETWEEN 17MAR89 AND 14APR89
SYSTEM = CPUA
LM
2%
TESTING
34%
MBTC
34%
OTHER PRODUCTION
5%
DATABASE
3%
OTHER
21%

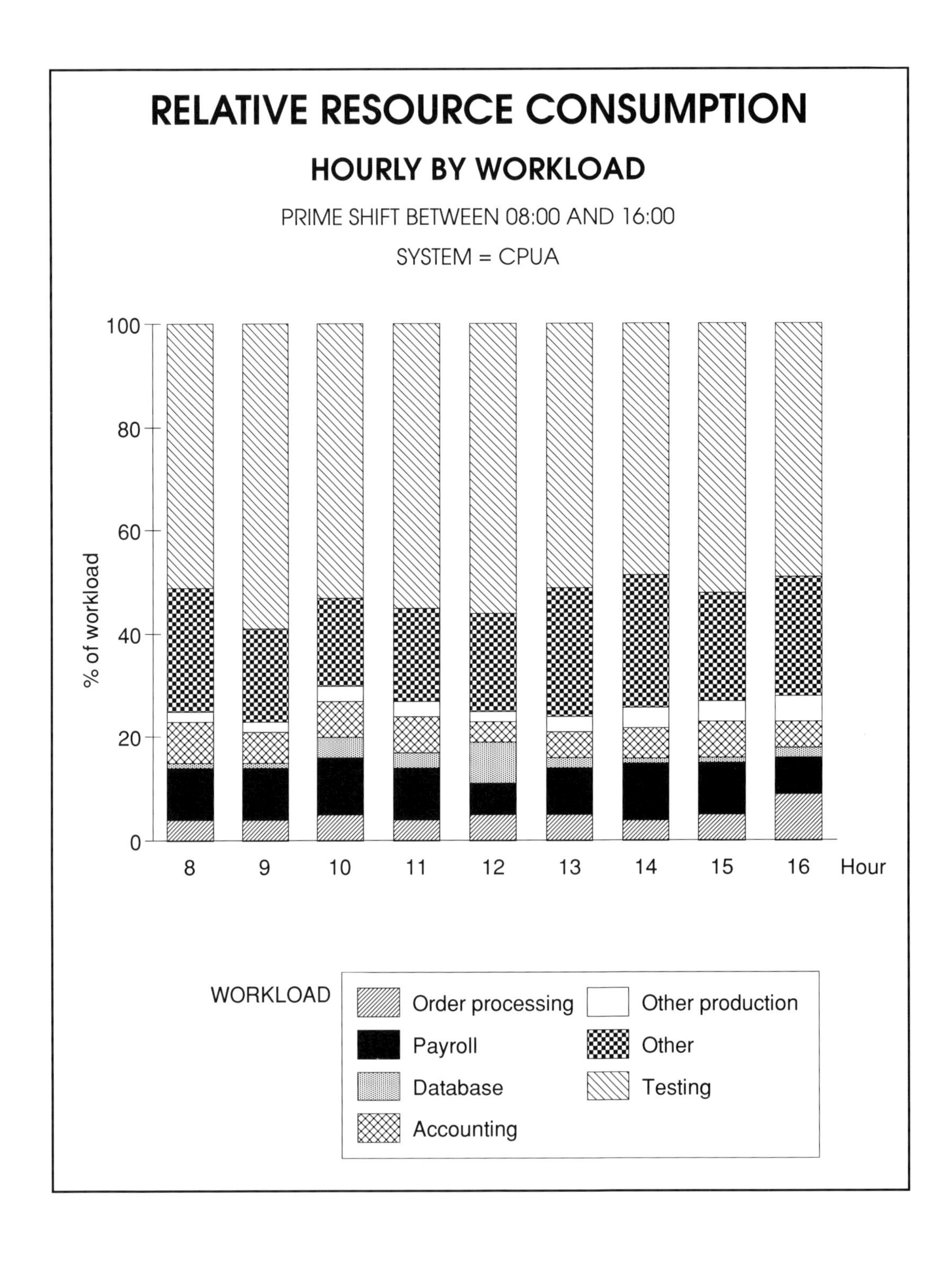
RELATIVE RESOURCE CONSUMPTION
HOURLY BY WORKLOAD
PRIME SHIFT BETWEEN 08:00 AND 16:00
SYSTEM = CPUA
% of workload
0
20
40
60
80
100
8
9
10
11
12
13
14
15
16
Hour
WORKLOAD
Order processing
Payroll
Database
Accounting
Other production
Other
Testing

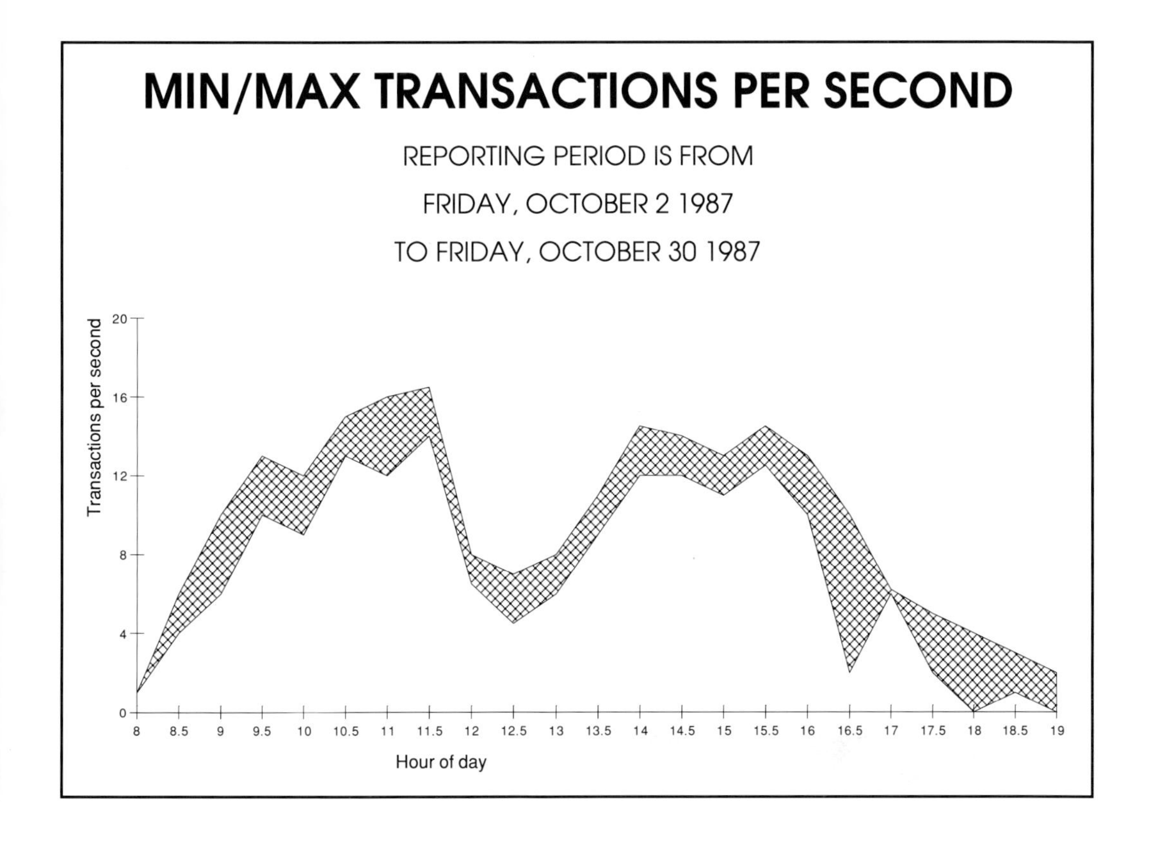
MIN/MAX TRANSACTIONS PER SECOND
REPORTING PERIOD IS FROM
FRIDAY, OCTOBER 2 1987
TO FRIDAY, OCTOBER 30 1987
Transactions per second
0
4
8
12
16
20
Hour of day
8
8.5
9
9.5
10
10.5
11
11.5
12
12.5
13
13.5
14
14.5
15
15.5
16
16.5
17
17.5
18
18.5
19

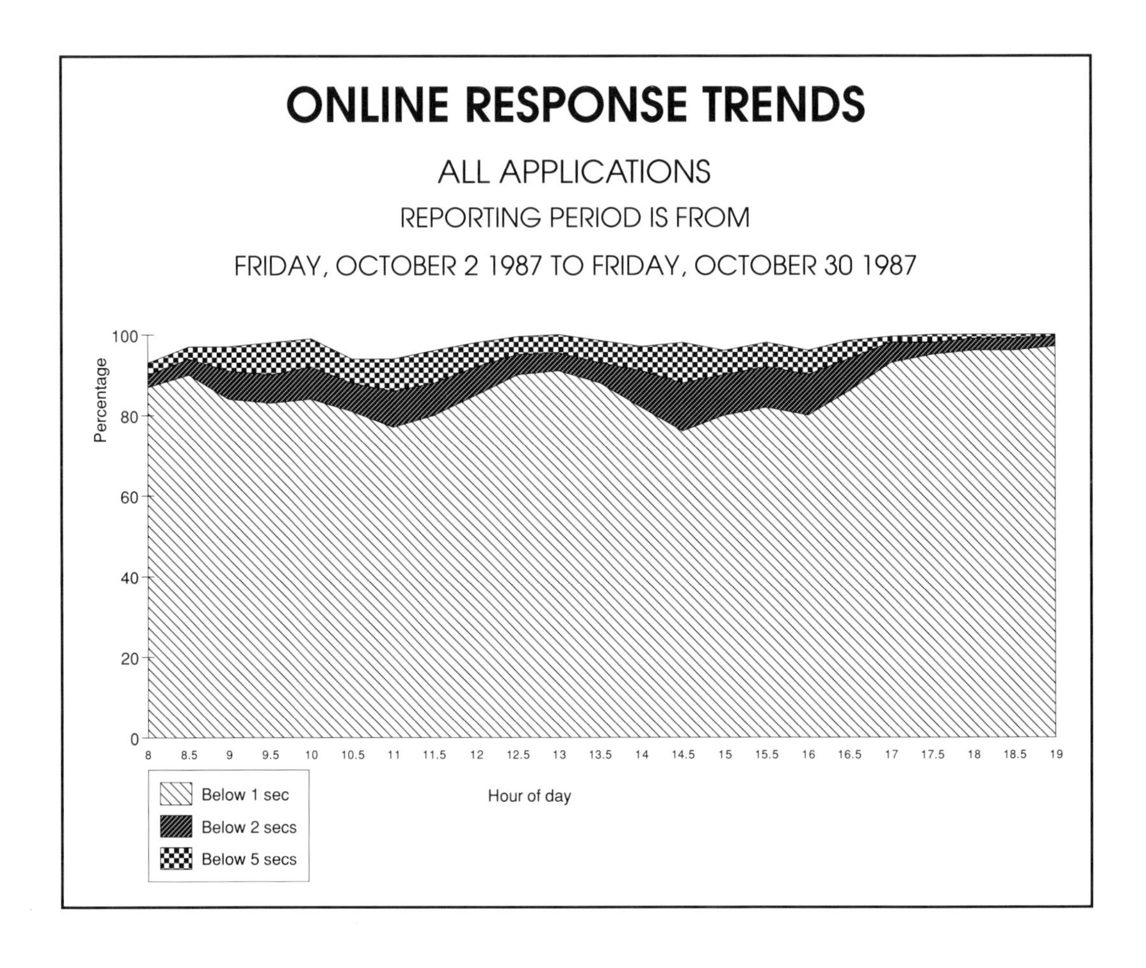
ONLINE RESPONSE TRENDS
ALL APPLICATIONS
REPORTING PERIOD IS FROM
FRIDAY, OCTOBER 2 1987 TO FRIDAY, OCTOBER 30 1987
Percentage
100
80
60
40
20
0
8
8.5
9
9.5
10
10.5
11
11.5
12
12.5
13
13.5
14
14.5
15
15.5
16
16.5
17
17.5
18
18.5
19
Hour of day
Below 1 sec
Below 2 secs
Below 5 secs

UTILIZATION STATISTICS - PRIME SHIFT

CHANNEL BUSY PEAK HOUR

FRIDAY, OCTOBER 2 1987

TO FRIDAY, OCTOBER 30 1987

COMPONENT	PEAK HOUR	% BUSY	10%ile	50 %ile	90 %ile	THRESHOLD VALUE	% TIME OVER THRESHOLD
CHAN 0A	11	19.97	12.47	19.72	28.57	30	6.25
CHAN 0B	11	19.97	11.91	19.50	28.15	30	6.25
CHAN04	11	23.38	16.73	22.59	30.14	30	12.50
CHAN05	11	22.11	15.23	21.61	30.05	30	10.00
CPU	11	80.99	67.78	81.52	94.14	100	0.00
PRINT A	11	49.73	6.89	49.75	92.22	75	26.47
PRINT B	11	61.37	7.12	75.72	99.50	75	50.00
TAPE	11	7.59	0.24	4.22	20.13	30	2.29

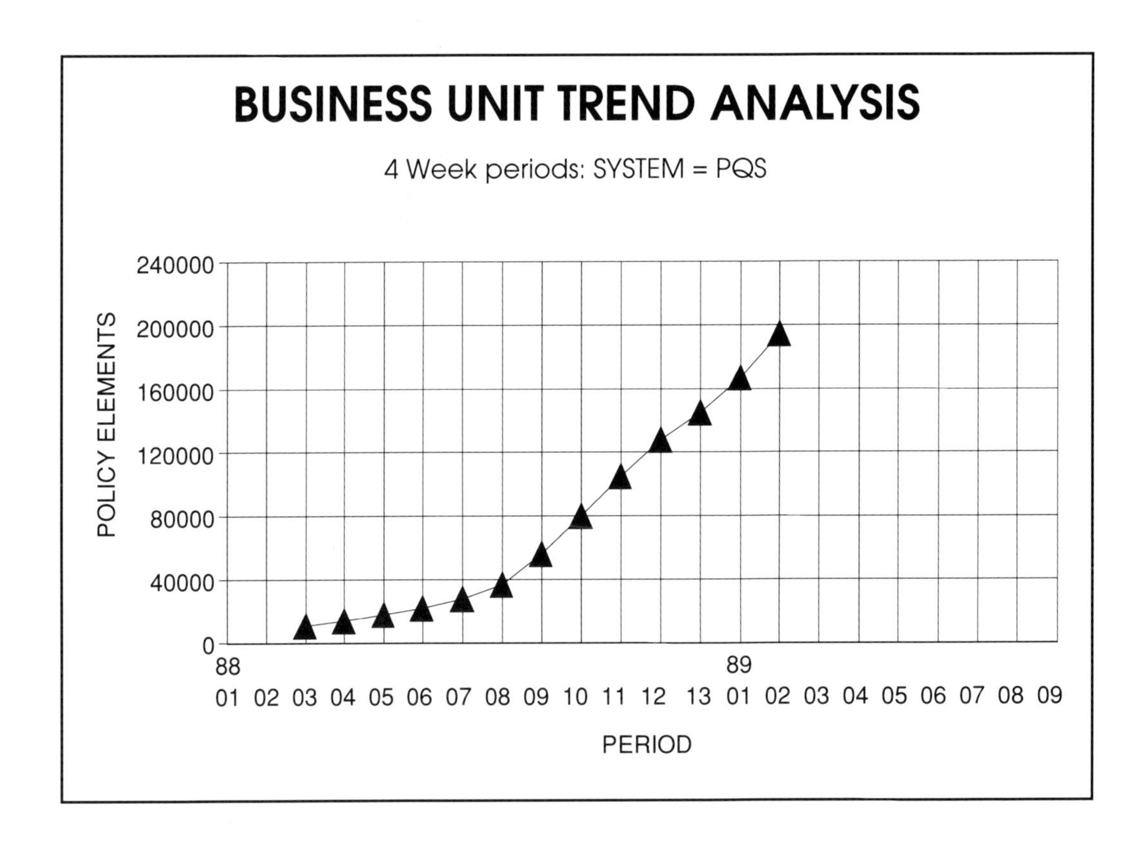
BUSINESS UNIT TREND ANALYSIS
4 Week periods: SYSTEM = PQS
POLICY ELEMENTS
240000
200000
160000
120000
80000
40000
0
88
89
01 02 03 04 05 06 07 08 09 10 11 12 13 01 02 03 04 05 06 07 08 09
PERIOD

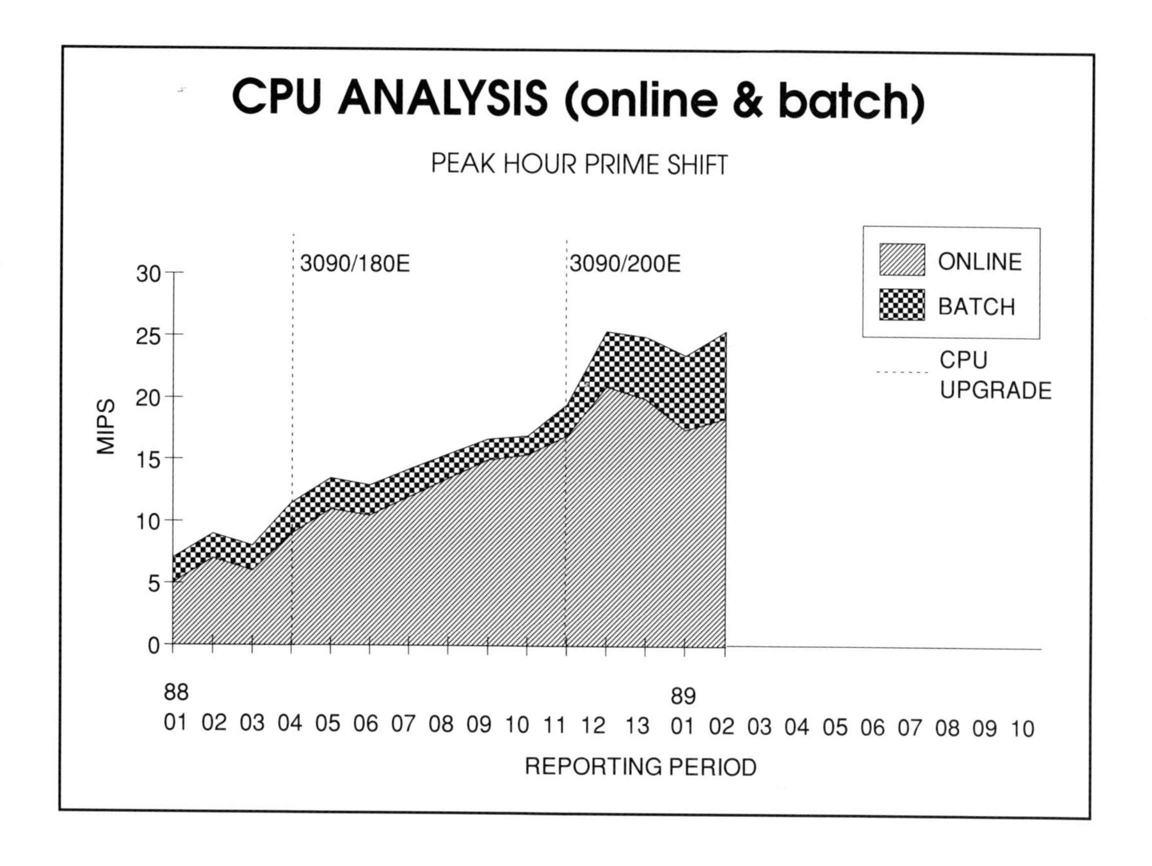
CPU ANALYSIS (online & batch)
PEAK HOUR PRIME SHIFT
3090/180E
3090/200E
ONLINE
BATCH
CPU UPGRADE
MIPS
30
25
20
15
10
5
0
88
89
01 02 03 04 05 06 07 08 09 10 11 12 13 01 02 03 04 05 06 07 08 09 10
REPORTING PERIOD

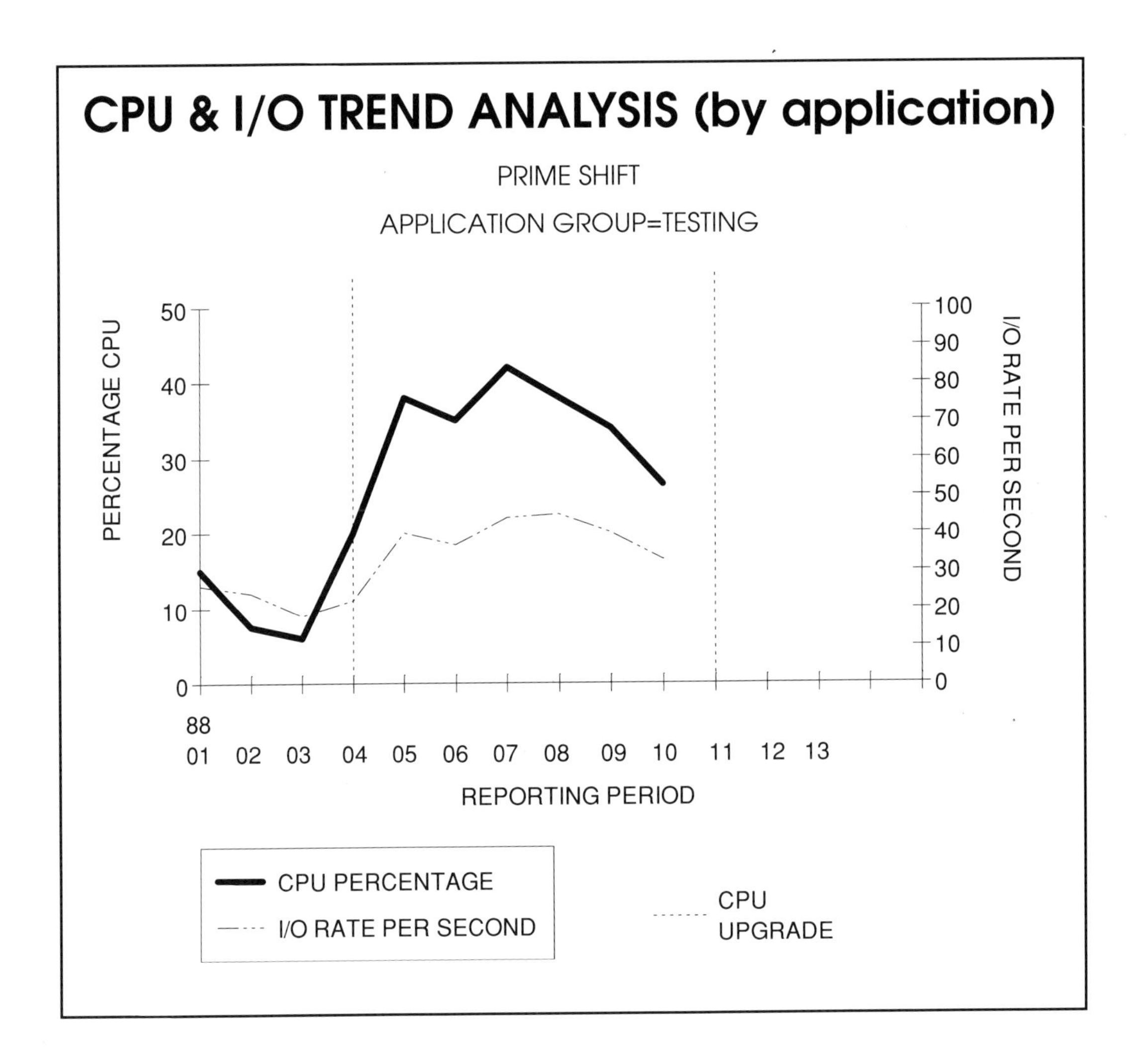
CPU & I/O TREND ANALYSIS (by application)
PRIME SHIFT
APPLICATION GROUP=TESTING
PERCENTAGE CPU
50
40
30
20
10
0
100
90
80
70
60
50
40
30
20
10
0
I/O RATE PER SECOND
88
01 02 03 04 05 06 07 08 09 10 11 12 13
REPORTING PERIOD
CPU PERCENTAGE
I/O RATE PER SECOND
CPU
UPGRADE

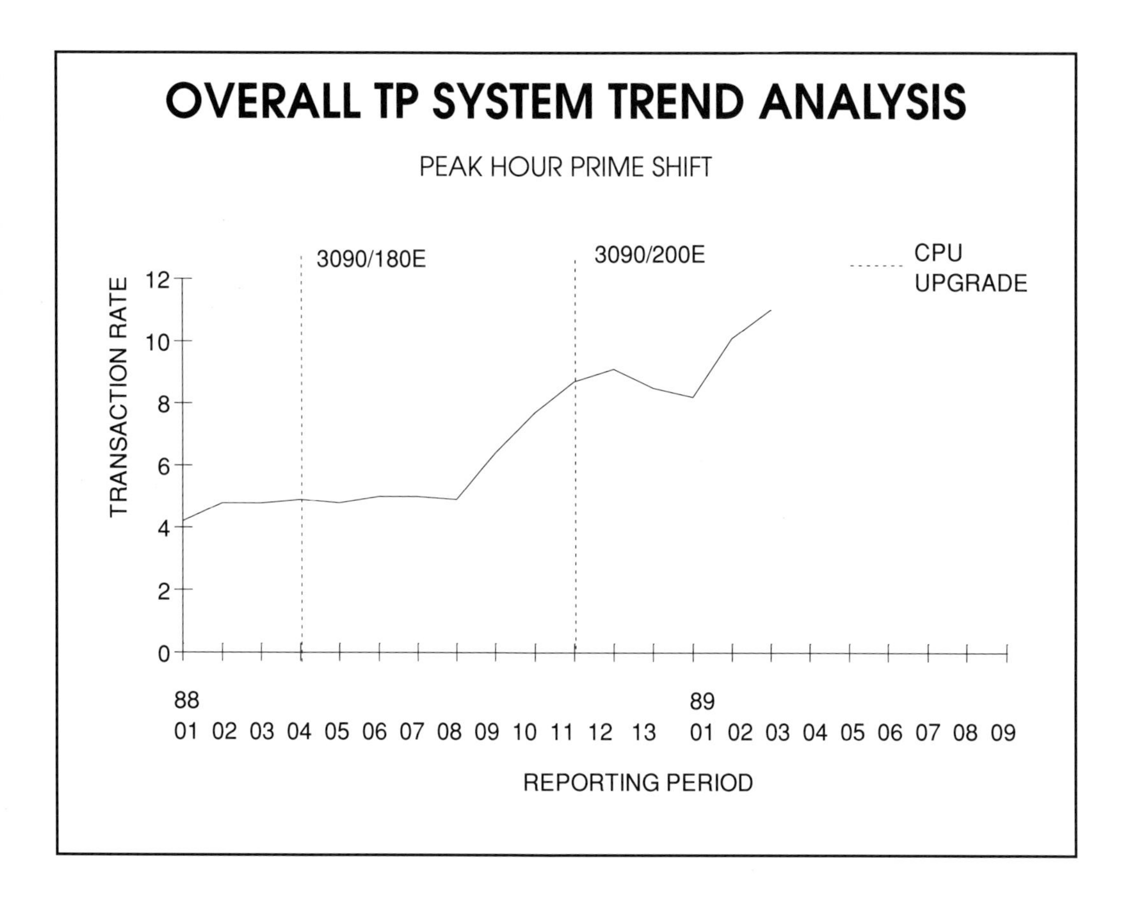
OVERALL TP SYSTEM TREND ANALYSIS
PEAK HOUR PRIME SHIFT
3090/180E
3090/200E
CPU UPGRADE
TRANSACTION RATE
0
2
4
6
8
10
12
88
89
01 02 03 04 05 06 07 08 09 10 11 12 13 01 02 03 04 05 06 07 08 09
REPORTING PERIOD

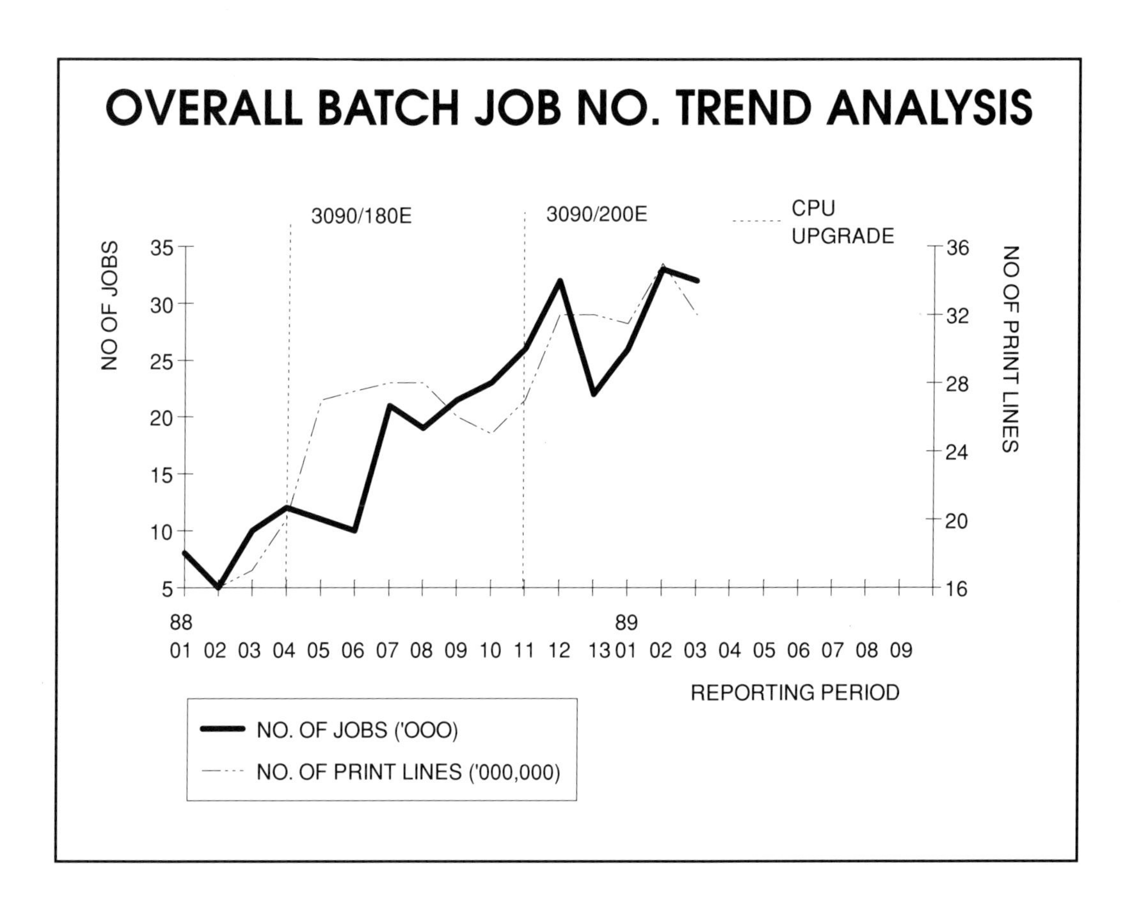
OVERALL BATCH JOB NO. TREND ANALYSIS
3090/180E
3090/200E
CPU UPGRADE
NO OF JOBS
35
30
25
20
15
10
5
NO OF PRINT LINES
36
32
28
24
20
16
88
89
01 02 03 04 05 06 07 08 09 10 11 12 13 01 02 03 04 05 06 07 08 09
REPORTING PERIOD
NO. OF JOBS ('OOO)
NO. OF PRINT LINES ('000,000)

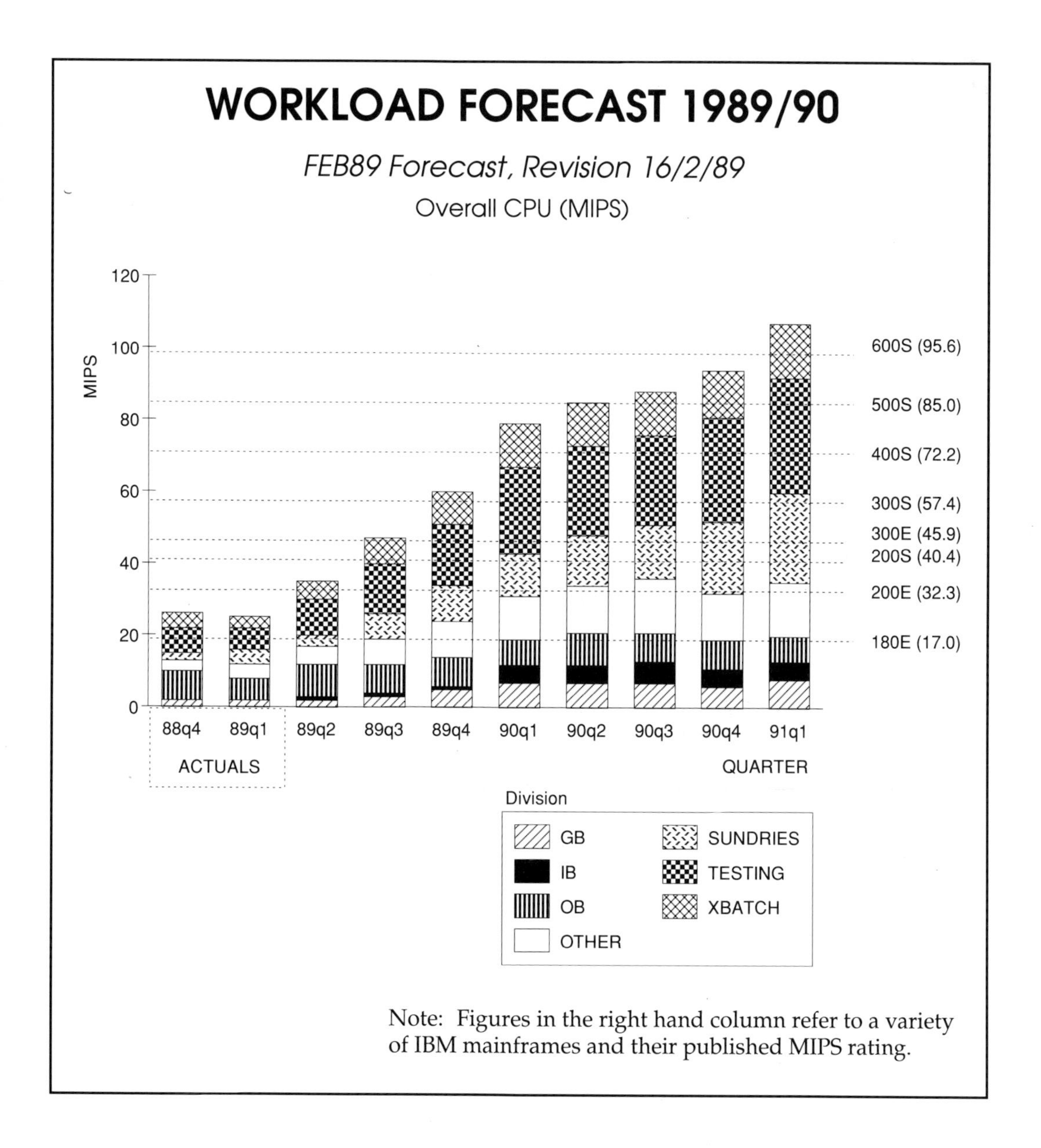

Note: Figures in the right hand column refer to a variety of IBM mainframes and their published MIPS rating.

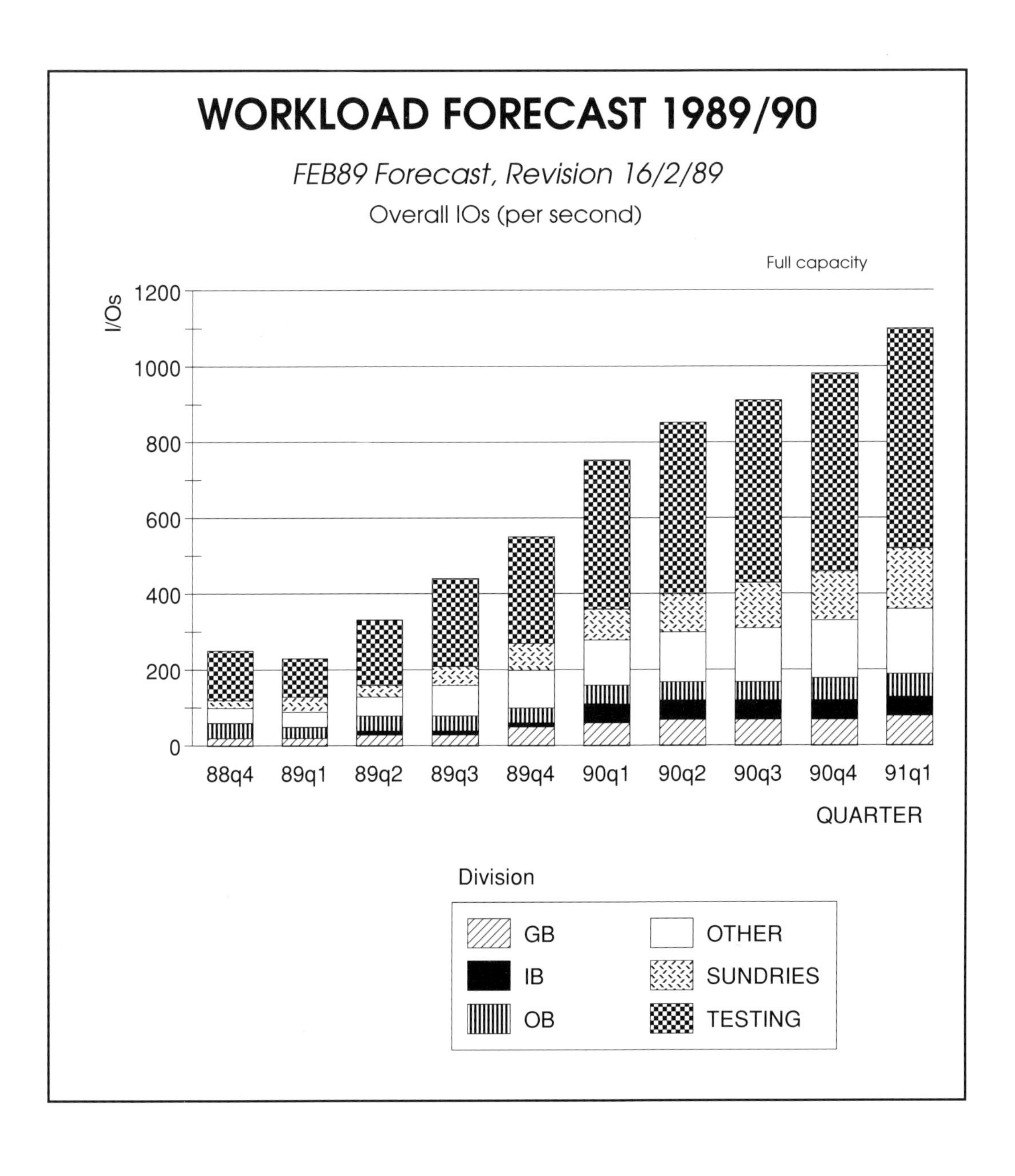
WORKLOAD FORECAST 1989/90
FEB89 Forecast, Revision 16/2/89
Overall IOs (per second)
Full capacity
I/Os
1200
1000
800
600
400
200
0
88q4
89q1
89q2
89q3
89q4
90q1
90q2
90q3
90q4
91q1
QUARTER
Division
GB
IB
OB
OTHER
SUNDRIES
TESTING

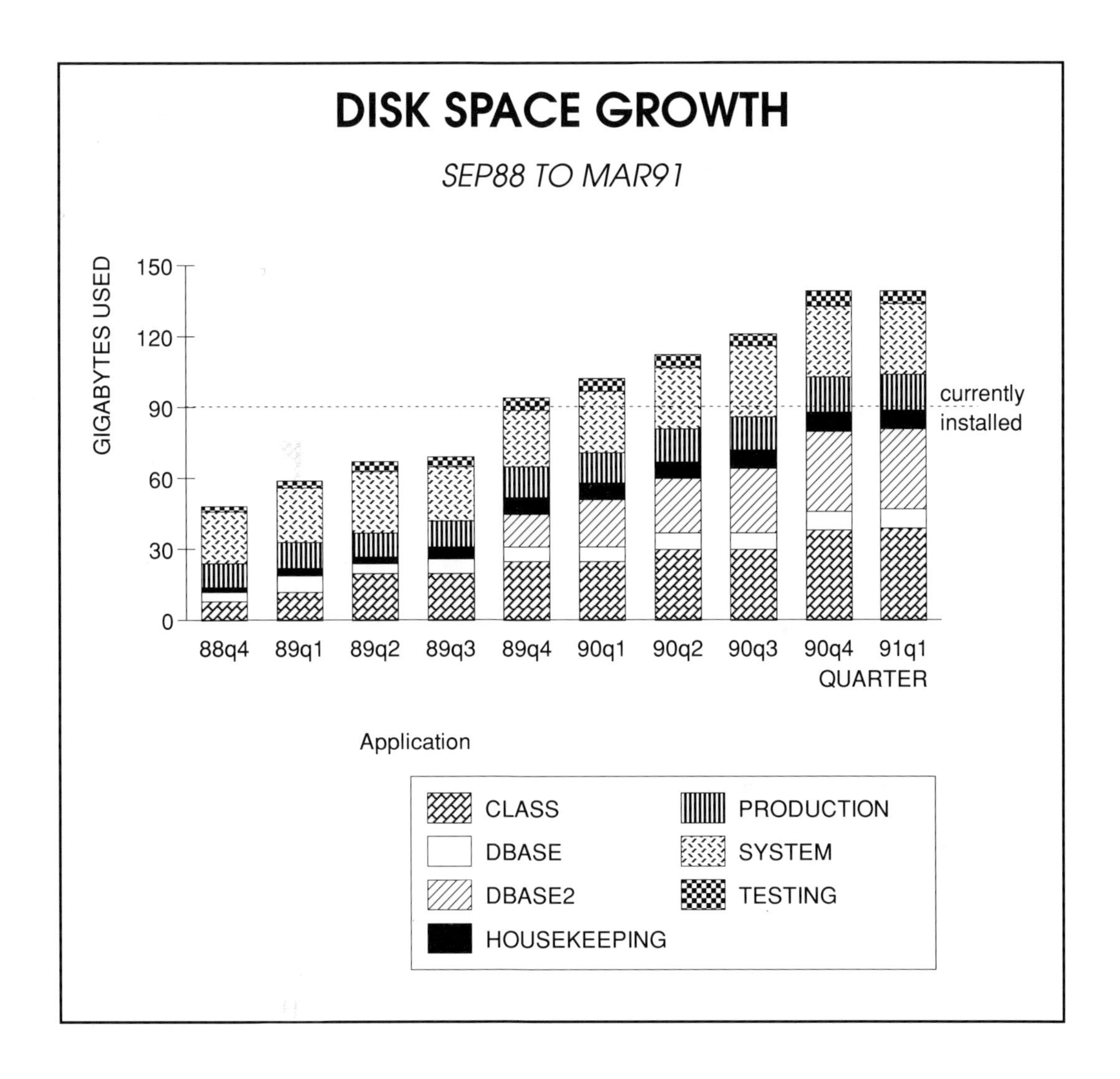
DISK SPACE GROWTH
SEP88 TO MAR91
GIGABYTES USED
150
120
90
60
30
0
currently
installed
88q4
89q1
89q2
89q3
89q4
90q1
90q2
90q3
90q4
91q1
QUARTER
Application
CLASS
DBASE
DBASE2
HOUSEKEEPING
PRODUCTION
SYSTEM
TESTING

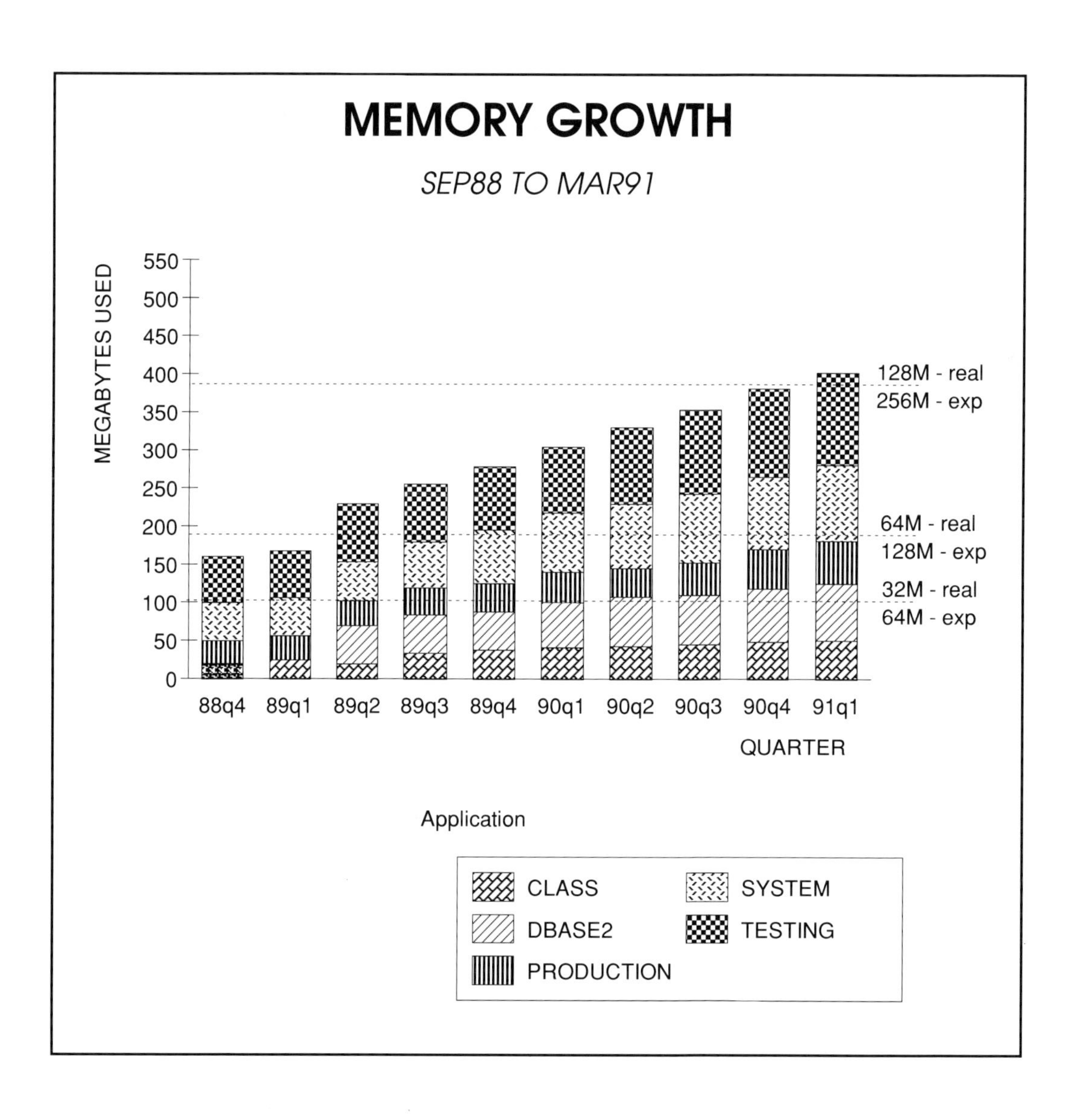
MEMORY GROWTH
SEP88 TO MAR91
MEGABYTES USED
550
500
450
400
350
300
250
200
150
100
50
0
128M - real
256M - exp
64M - real
128M - exp
32M - real
64M - exp
88q4
89q1
89q2
89q3
89q4
90q1
90q2
90q3
90q4
91q1
QUARTER
Application
CLASS
SYSTEM
DBASE2
TESTING
PRODUCTION

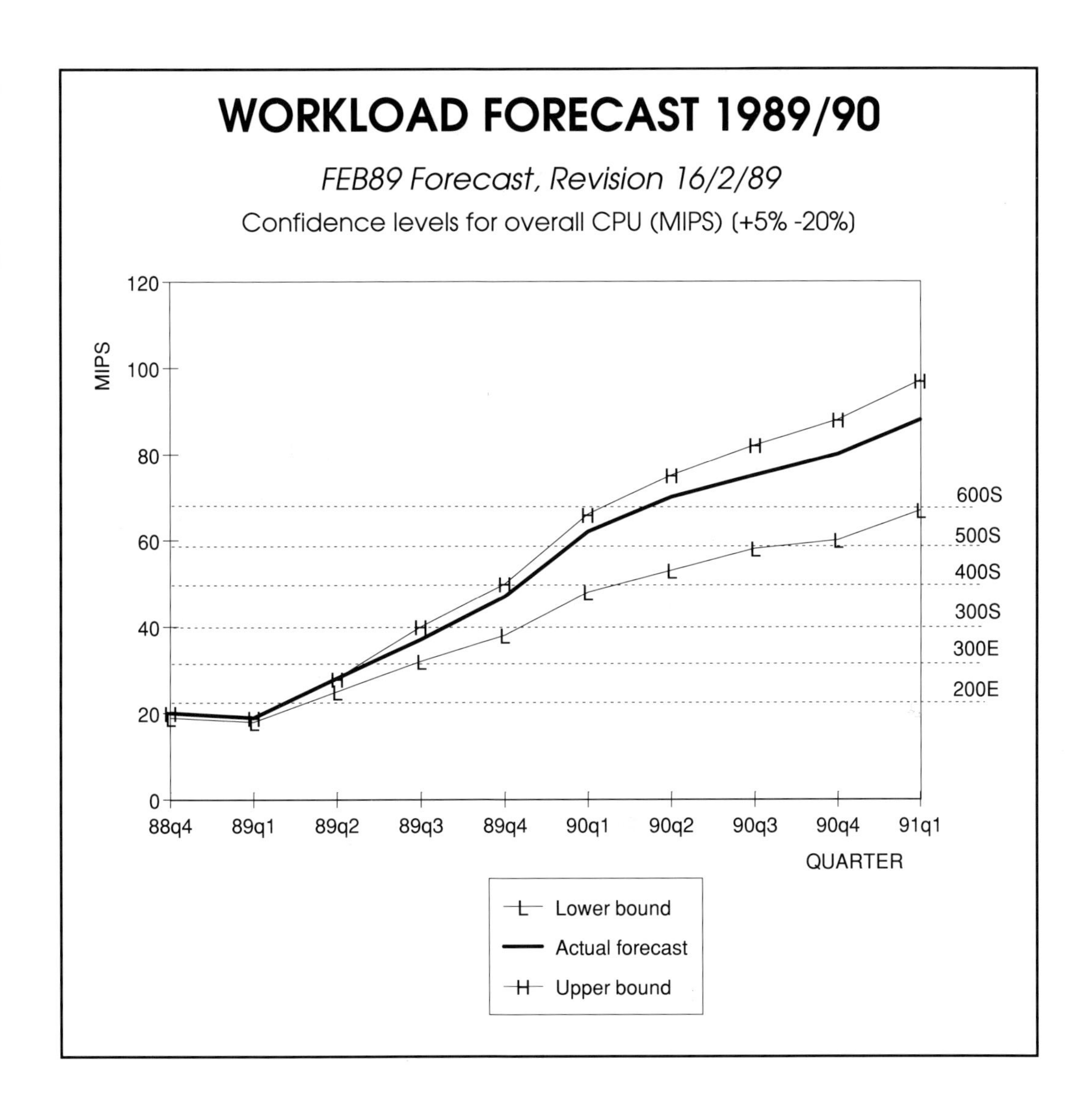
WORKLOAD FORECAST 1989/90
FEB89 Forecast, Revision 16/2/89
Confidence levels for overall CPU (MIPS) (+5% -20%)
MIPS
120
100
80
60
40
20
0
600S
500S
400S
300S
300E
200E
88q4
89q1
89q2
89q3
89q4
90q1
90q2
90q3
90q4
91q1
QUARTER
Lower bound
Actual forecast
Upper bound

CCTA hopes that you find this book both useful and interesting. We will welcome your comments and suggestions for improving it.
Please use this form or a photocopy, and continue on a further sheet if needed.

From:

Name

Organization

Address

Telephone

COVERAGE
Does the material cover your needs?
If not, then what additional material would you like included.

CLARITY
Are there any points which are unclear?
If yes, please detail where and why.

ACCURACY
Please give details of any inaccuracies found.

If more space is required for these or other comments, please continue overleaf.

OTHER COMMENTS

Return to:

Library
CCTA
Rosebery Court
St Andrews Business Park
Norwich NR7 0HS

Further information

For further information regarding this publication and other CCTA products please contact:

Library
CCTA
Rosebery Court
St Andrews Business Park
Norwich NR7 0HS

01603 704930

The price of this publication has been set to make a contribution to the costs incurred by CCTA in preparing the copy.

Printed in the United Kingdom for The Stationery Office
TJ000547 2/00 C6 10170